8971

THE OPERATIONAL CODE OF THE POLITBURO

The RAND Series

This is one of a series of publications which will present results of research undertaken by The RAND Corporation, a nonprofit organization, chartered "to further and promote scientific, educational, and charitable purposes, all for the public welfare and security of the United States of America."

THE OPERATIONAL CODE
OF
THE POLITBURO

Nathan Leites

The RAND Corporation

First Edition

GREENWOOD PRESS, PUBLISHERS
WESTPORT, CONNECTICUT

The Library of Congress has catalogued this publication as follows:

Library of Congress Cataloging in Publication Data

Leites, Nathan Constantin, 1912–
    The operational code of the Politburo.

    Original ed. issued in the Rand series.
    Bibliography: p.
    1. Kommunisticheskaia partiia Sovetskogo Soiuza.
TSentral nyi Komitet. Politicheskoe Biuro. I. Title.
II. Series.
[JN6598.K7L37   1972]   329.9'47   73-140652
ISBN 0-8371-5812-5

Originally published in 1951
by McGraw-Hill, New York

Reprinted with the permission
of The Rand Corporation

First Greenwood Reprinting 1972

Library of Congress Catalogue Card Number 73-140652

ISBN 0-8371-5812-5

Printed in the United States of America

Author's Note

THE points developed in this volume have been influenced by numerous discussions with Elsa Bernaut, Margaret Mead, and Martha Wolfenstein. Susan Viton worked untiringly on the editing of the various drafts. I would like to express my particular debt to the following among my colleagues on the staff of The RAND Corporation who contributed guidance and suggestions during the preparation of the final manuscript: Hans Speier, Joseph M. Goldsen, Herbert Goldhamer, Victor M. Hunt, Paul Kecskemeti, Raymond L. Garthoff, and Philip Selznick.

NATHAN LEITES

NEW YORK CITY
December 1, 1950

Foreword

THIS book is the first of a series of monographs in which the results of research by members of the staff of The RAND Corporation will be made available to the public.

The author of this volume, Dr. Nathan Leites, began the present study while a research associate of the National Policy Committee at Yale University, under the financial sponsorship of the Carnegie Corporation of New York. The study is being continued by The RAND Corporation as a part of its program of research for the United States Air Force.

This short guide to Politburo behavior, summarizing the provisional findings of a continuing investigation, is being published at this time because of the growing interest in this subject and its importance to every responsible citizen. It is hoped that other students of Soviet affairs will examine the rules of Soviet political conduct suggested in this book and test them against actual political and military events.

Contents

Introduction

THIS book presents some of the findings of a still-continuing study of the political strategy of Bolshevism and is based on the writings of Lenin and Stalin.

The intention is not to discuss the major theories of Leninism-Stalinism but to discover the rules which Bolsheviks believe to be necessary for effective political conduct. Although a number of these rules, stated in a general form, can be found throughout Bolshevik literature, many others have only been implied in the political analyses made by Bolsheviks within the last half-century. An attempt has been made to draw explicit and systematic formulations from this wealth of data and to set them down within a meaningful frame of reference. This book deals mainly with the relations between the Party and the outside world rather than with the Party's internal relations. Unless otherwise stated, the rules given below are believed to apply (in varying degrees) to both the Leninist and the Stalinist eras of Bolshevism.

The present study is limited to a formulation of the significant rules for which evidence has so far been found and to some illustrations drawn from that evidence. It does not indicate the various elements out of which the Bolsheviks have constructed these rules; that is to say, there is no discussion of the degree to which they may have been influenced by the spirit of a Westernized Russian intelligentsia, by Marxism, or by the need to adapt such rules to particular power situations.

A subsequent study will contain complete documentation of the Bolshevik and Western sources used in the study. The rules governing relations within the Party, as well as with the outside world, will be discussed; an attempt will be made to show how Bolshevik conceptions are related to Russian and

Western history and culture; and the manifold connections between the various aspects of the Bolshevik attitude toward
politics will be examined, as well as the changes in it effected
by time.

The rules cited in this study fall into three categories. Some
have been explicitly stated by Lenin and Stalin and appear as
direct quotations from their writings. Some are so clearly
implied for specific situations that Bolsheviks would easily recognize them as they appear below. Others seem to be operative
among Bolsheviks but might not be recognized easily by them.

For the sake of clarity, the *general rules* of Bolshevik conduct
are given in full-width text and the *examples* illustrating them,
in indented text. Throughout, statements have been constructed
using words and phrases from the writings and speeches of
Lenin and Stalin. This results in statements which may often
be imperfect, or contradictory, from a scientific point of view,
but which do represent an actual pattern of Bolshevik thought.
For the same reason, in grouping these rules into chapters, the
repetition and overlapping which has developed has not been
eliminated. Indeed, the lack of codification by the Bolsheviks
not only makes such imperfections inevitable, but, from an
analytic point of view, makes them significant.

As the lack of frankness in Bolshevik public statements has
sharply increased with the passage of time, the frequent use
of examples remote in time and in subject matter could not
be avoided.

Because of the special position of the Party in Bolshevik
doctrine, it is to the Party rather than to the Soviet government
that the rules are said to apply.

Each point should be evaluated in its total context rather
than separately.

It is not assumed that any of the rules cited apply exclusively
to the Bolsheviks. Many of them are held by other ruling groups
in the present or have been held in the past. It is only the entire
code which is characteristic of Bolshevism.

On the other hand, there is reason to assume that these rules are pervasive in Bolshevik policy calculations, whether they refer to domestic or foreign policy, propaganda, or military policy.

A number of items in the code are used not only as guides to action, but also as guidance for propaganda. This study is concerned only with policy calculations.

* * *

To ensure the best predictions of Politburo action, many kinds of data besides the writings of Lenin and Stalin should be analyzed. The historical record reveals unverbalized, but equally important, rules of conduct of this group of policy-makers. It may also reveal a disposition to deviate from recognized rules under certain conditions. Further, only an analysis of the historical record can contribute answers to the following questions: When the operational code specifies that there is an optimal degree for a certain kind of behavior, intermediate between too much and too little (e.g., Chap. XI, pars. 1 and 2), what is that optimum for a certain period and area? And when the operational code permits the application of two or more contrasting rules to a certain situation (e.g., Chap. XVI, pars. 5 and 9), what are the factors determining the choice?

But even in a full analysis the kind of inquiry reported on here would be important for the following reasons:

1. The Politburo has, until now, maintained an attitude of extreme reserve and deceptiveness toward the outside world. The poker face, the exuberant cordiality of the nth vodka-toast, and the storm of indignation from the U.N. rostrum are all designed to conceal the real Soviet aim from the enemy (and who is not a potential enemy?). As a result, even persons who have had considerable direct contact with Soviet policy-makers have had to turn to the Soviet doctrinal texts for aid in prediction.[1]

2. Most, perhaps all, of the members of the Politburo started

---

For footnotes, see pp. 91–95.

their careers as devotees of a secular religion. It is possible that their religious fervor has declined with time, but it would probably be wrong to regard them as being mainly cynical. Hence, a study of the sacred texts of Bolshevism—the works of Lenin and Stalin—seems necessary if we want to increase our skill in predicting Politburo behavior. These texts are particularly useful because they are concerned primarily with the strategy and tactics of socialism-communism, and very little with its virtues and advantages, which are taken for granted.

Since the Politburo has abandoned the unusual frankness in statements of policy that existed up to about 1930, any conclusions concerning present rules of strategy of the Politburo must remain, to some extent, conjectural. But it seems likely that the Politburo today is even more strongly bound by tradition to its system of operation than to its conception of a communist society. This seemed to appear in the letters (highly classified when they were written) addressed by the Moscow Poltiburo in 1948 to its Belgrade counterpart,[2] which showed little variation from earlier patterns of argumentation. Likewise, the themes developed in the 1949 trials of Laszlo Rajk and Traicho Kostov were very similar to those of the Moscow trials in the thirties (particularly to the last trial in March, 1938) and may indicate the persistence of certain conceptions —e.g., concerning espionage—determining these public themes.

3. It is likely that the Politburo considers the record of the Soviet regime to be largely one of success, and that a large part of this success is attributed to the use of "correct" rules of strategy (as expounded in the Lenin-Stalin texts) which, therefore, should continue to be followed. In 1920, Lenin said:

> There can be no question but that we have learned politics;
> we cannot be misled here; here we have a basis.[3]

Many of these rules of strategy were developed early in the history of Bolshevism during the struggles among the small groups of Russian Socialists. In 1922, Lenin said:

... we have experienced bourgeois diplomacy. It is the sort of thing the Mensheviks taught us for fifteen years.[4]

It is also likely that the present Politburo still believes a contemporary situation in international affairs to be explainable when its prototype can be found in Russian, or Party, history. Thus Stalin wrote in 1938:

... the ruling circles of Britain are roughly pursuing the same policy as was pursued under tsardom by the Russian liberal-monarchist bourgeois, who, while fearing the "excesses" of tsarist policy, feared the people even more, and therefore resorted to a policy of pleading with the tsar and, consequently, of conspiring with the tsar against the people.[5]

And in 1949, when the Soviet government protested to Yugoslavia against an alleged maltreatment of Soviet nationals, it based its case on a comparison of the Stockholm Congress of the Russian Social Democratic Labor Party in 1906 with the London Congress of 1907.

Bolshevik attitudes toward power have not undergone any basic change since the conquest of power in Russia (or outside of Russia since 1939). Before the Revolution, the Bolsheviks had attempted to gain power in Russia and to escape the sanctions of its rulers. Since the Revolution, they have continued to see themselves in the same position in relation to the outside world as they were in relation to the tsarist government, i.e., out of power and in a dangerous position. Thus, the world-revolutionary aims of the Bolsheviks tend to preserve the importance of the lessons they learned in their earlier struggles.

This study does not attempt to analyze recent or current Politburo behavior in terms of the policy rules which are described. However, at the end of each chapter there is a brief statement with a few suggestions in this direction. These suggestions are *simply hypotheses* and further research is needed to test them. Moreover, they are *merely illustrative;* they cover only a very small part of the range of application of the rules stated.

THE OPERATIONAL CODE
OF
THE POLITBURO

CHAPTER 1

PREDICTABILITY AND UNPREDICTABILITY

1. One point of Bolshevik doctrine affirms that future developments are either inevitable or impossible. Intermediate probabilities are excluded. This is a characteristic "all-or-none" pattern of Bolshevik thought.

2. A Bolshevik may regard the statement that "A is compatible with B" as being equivalent to "A follows from B."

In an intense and protracted fight by Lenin against positivism (the results of which have become basic to Bolshevik philosophy), his opponents' point—that science cannot disprove religion—meant to him that they were advocating religion.

3. All politically important events are explainable by the laws of Marxism-Leninism. Therefore, no such event is "accidental." Only "political philistines" regard such an event as the result of some force other than that determining the transition of society from capitalism to communism.

4. All the actors on the world scene are "forced" into their parts through the pressure of historical developments. Only the Party, through its insight and dedication, acts freely.

The "masses" put themselves under the leadership of the Party when it becomes "intolerable" or "impossible" to "go on living in the old way." Enemies make concessions only when they are "forced" to do so, when they are "pushed" into doing so "against their own wishes," by the pressure of the Party, or the masses, or other circumstances.

5. When the Party carries out a correct line, it "does not invent" anything, but acts strictly in accordance with what is prescribed by the historical situation. The Party "solves the problem that has been put on the agenda by history."

1

6. Despite such beliefs in determinism, Bolshevik doctrine also contains contrasting points. Thus, although it is always asserted that the direction and end of a major historical development (e.g., the transition from capitalism to communism) is predictable, the length of time and the path such a development will take are not held to be predictable.

In 1918, during the debates on the Brest-Litovsk peace, Lenin pointed out that the "Left Communists" were in error, not in predicting a German revolution but in assigning a date to it.

7. "It is impossible to have a plan completed in advance" for a whole historical period. "The new tasks originate when we work on solving the old ones." "Napoleon . . . wrote . . .: One must first start a serious engagement and then see what happens."

In 1923, Lenin wrote:

Well, we started a serious engagement in . . . 1917, and then we saw such details of development (from the point of view of world history they are certainly details) as the Brest-Litovsk peace, the New Economic Policy, etc.[6]

8. It is not possible to predict when Communist victory on a world scale will be achieved (i.e., after how many decades, depressions, wars, and revolutions).

9. The Party must not fall into despair if certain gains take much longer than had been estimated. On a historical scale, such differences in rate of development are minor.

10. However, it is a task of the Party to shorten as much as possible the road to (and hence the cost of) victory.

11. This can be done because at many historical junctures more than one outcome is "objectively possible." "Objective conditions" create certain "opportunities" for the Party; whether the Party will succeed in "utilizing" them and transforming them into "realities" cannot be predicted.

12. The line of the Party at any given moment "must be realizable only in that . . . sense of the term that not a single

letter . . . should be counter to the direction of . . . socio-
economic development. Once we have correctly ascertained
this direction . . . we must . . . fight . . . with all our
forces for the maximum of our demands. It is philistine to
attempt to say in advance, before the . . . issue of the battle
. . . that we shall not reach the . . . maximum." That is, the
"relationship of forces" which determines the outcome can only
be ascertained by the test of battle (whether violent or not).

> Thus, the "periodic redivisions of the world" in the
> era of imperialism "can proceed only by violence, by
> testing the power of the various groups of imperialist
> countries."

Similarly, as to the course of a protracted "battle," "only agitation is able to show us the real mood of the masses . . . [to]
furnish us faultless material for the ascertainment of the tempo
of the maturing of the conditions for . . . more decisive
struggles."

> In 1917, Lenin affirmed that it is "the major task of
> the day" to "destroy the confidence" of the masses in
> those socialists who did not oppose the war. He said:

> > How realizable from the point of view of the mood of the
> > . . . masses such a policy is can only be *proved* by a most . . .
> > energetic approach to such an agitation. . . .[7]

13. Although a Bolshevik holds that the outcome of a crucial
situation may be indeterminate, he also affirms the number of
possible "solutions" to be very small, since Marxism-Leninism
shows that many possibilities (e.g., the peaceful surrender of
power on the part of a "ruling class") believed in by "political
philistines" "do not exist in nature at all."

*   *   *

Consistent with par. 3, the Politburo in its interpretations of
the world outside often seems to perceive connections between
events where we see none; to regard unrelated details as symp-
tomatic of major political trends; and to believe that there is

complicated planning behind events which we know to be fortuitous.

Consistent with par. 6, the Politburo belief in their correct insight into the laws of history is compatible with their lack of certainty as to how even the most decisive events of the times are going to turn out. During the period between 1936 and 1942, the Politburo presumably regarded as possible a new conflict between the two enemy blocs, with the Soviet Union staying out at least until the final phase; or the establishment of an Anglo-American hegemony in the world outside the Soviet Union; or an Anglo-German bloc in Europe. It is likely that the developments which actually occurred were not specifically predicted in Moscow, where a sharp decline in British power and a coalition between the Soviet Union and other major powers appeared as improbable. But it is almost certain that when this happened, the Politburo did not feel that their predictive skill had failed them.

Thus, consistent with pars. 6 and 7, Politburo calculations are marked both by a deliberate orientation toward the future and by a flexible taking-into-account of immediate contingencies.

Consistent with pars. 8 and 9, the Politburo is willing to bide its time indefinitely.

On the one hand, the Politburo is secure in its belief in the correctness of its operations, as being grounded in fact (pars. 4 and 5); on the other hand, its motivation to try as hard as possible to ensure success for its aims is reinforced by pars. 10, 11, and 12.

In a novel situation, like that created by the development of nuclear physics, the Politburo tends to avoid facing the necessity for radical, social inventions by stressing the Marxist-Leninist laws of history (pars. 3 and 13). Although the Politburo is realistic in dealing with the immediate consequences, military and industrial, of new technologies, it tends to feel that the essentials in human affairs—seen in terms of "capitalism," "socialism," "communism"—have not changed.

CHAPTER 2
ORIENTATION ON THE PAST AND TOWARD THE FUTURE

1. All events, foreign as well as domestic, must be viewed in the light of Party history, particularly of its early phases. The real nature of a contemporary event is considered to be revealed when its antecedent has been found in Party history; i.e., if the new situation can be shown to differ little or not at all from one that has already occurred in the Party's past.

In 1918, Lenin quoted predictions made by Engels in 1887 and said:

> ... what is most astonishing is that so many of Engels' predictions are turning out "according to the book." For Engels gave a perfectly exact class analysis, and classes in their mutual relations have remained unchanged.[8]

Early in 1948, Moscow equated the Yugoslav deviation with the "revisionist" trend in the German Social Democratic Party at the turn of the century; with the "liquidators" in the Russian Social Democratic Party in 1908–1914; and with the "Trotskyites" as well as the "Rights" in the Communist Party of the Soviet Union (CPSU) in the late 1920's. When the Yugoslav leaders denied the relevance of some of these comparisons, Moscow answered:

> Comrades Tito and Kardelj state that the errors of the Mensheviks regarding the merging of the Marxist party into a non-party mass organization were committed forty years ago and therefore can have no connection with the present mistakes of the Politburo of the Central Committee of the Communist Party of Yugoslavia. Comrades Tito and Kardelj are profoundly mistaken. There can be no doubt of the . . . connection between these two events. . . .[9]

5

2. However, for Bolsheviks, only the history of the Party can serve to point out the future; in general (i.e., for other groups), the past is merely a record of decrepitude and death.

* * *

Western policy-makers who come in contact with Politburo members may best be able to determine their most useful line of policy if they fully realize the very special past to which the Politburo feels itself to be attached. American and, say, Italian policy-makers have widely differing political traditions, but an agreement between them on which have been the important events and precedents during the last half-century would be more easily reached than a similar agreement between American and Soviet policy-makers. Also, the Politburo member probably believes that he knows all that is necessary about the background of his opponents but that they do not know very much about the Bolshevik political past which he regards as so significant.

CHAPTER 3
MEANS AND ENDS

1. The ethics underlying Bolshevik behavior are rarely made explicit.

2. The fundamental law is to do all that enhances the power of the Party, the great and only instrument in the realization of communism, the great and only goal.

In 1920, Lenin said:

> Our morality is deduced from the class struggle of the proletariat. . . . Communist morality is the morality which serves this struggle. . . .[10]

That is, in view of the supreme moral goal (the transformation of man's destiny through communism), the only permissible question about any policy under consideration by the Party is: Will it enhance the power of the Party?

Hence, the Party "does not tie its hands, it does not restrict its activities to some preconceived . . . method of political struggle: it recognizes all methods of struggle as long as they . . . facilitate the achievement of the best results possible under the given conditions."

"Bourgeois" governments follow the same rule; but "petty bourgeois" governments are likely to be doctrinaire and hence weak and contemptible.

The Party, which must have "a political approach to everything," must also assume that every aspect of itself and of its environment can be "utilized" for the enhancement of its power unless there is conclusive evidence to the contrary.

3. Party policy must not be influenced by feelings or moral considerations. The sin of "putting political questions on a sentimental basis" leads to failure and, eventually (if not immediately), to annihilation. A "real" Bolshevik Party finds

it easy to conduct an expedient policy, which from a "senti-mental" point of view would be extremely repulsive (e.g., breaking a strike). A real Bolshevik Party knows that such contingencies will occur with increasing frequency as the Party's power increases. "A Communist who says that one should never dirty one's hands . . . that he is going to build a Communist society with clean . . . hands, is an empty phrasemonger."

In 1925, Stalin said about the reintroduction of a government monopoly in vodka:

> A great many people seem to believe that we can build socialism while we are wearing kid gloves. That is a great mistake, comrades. If we cannot get any loans . . . and if . . . we do not wish to become the enslaved debtors of the western European capitalists . . . then we must find other sources of income. . . . We have to make a choice between . . . slavery and vodka."[11]

It is held that "bourgeois" governments follow the same rule.

4. The Party must take account of the moral values held by those outside of it (or by its imperfect members) as political facts: "We conduct our . . . struggle . . . within certain limits for reasons of expediency. Under any given conditions we do not admit any actions which might disorganize our side or facilitate the assault of the enemy against us at a moment advantageous to him. . . . Let us suppose that the 'moral sense' of the . . . petty-bourgeois masses is outraged by the blows received by a strikebreaker. . . . In such a case we shall not agitate in favor of active violence [against strikebreakers], as that would be inexpedient for our struggle. But we shall not have 'respect' for the petty-bourgeois feelings. . . ."

5. During the advance toward communism, the Party must not strive for the immediate achievement of the ultimate aims of communism—e.g., mass welfare—except as a means of enhancing Party power. To do so would jeopardize the realization of communism.

In 1933, Stalin said:

> From the point of view of Leninism, collective farms . . .
> are a weapon and a weapon only.[12]

6. Bolsheviks do not consider that the chances of attaining certain goals may be lessened by the protracted, large-scale use of means which are at extreme variance to them, and this problem is rarely mentioned.

Lenin upheld such a policy for action directed mainly against the enemy; Stalin upholds it for action taken against the "masses" and the Party.

7. In choosing between two courses of action, one of which is manifestly "revolutionary" whereas the other is not, the Party should be guided by expediency only, rather than "be carried away" by a "romantic" attachment to revolutionary methods as such. Those who "turn up their noses at a modest . . . task which does not promise any . . . conspicuousness . . . right away are not revolutionaries, but just ranters"; for the "greatest danger . . . is exaggeration of revolutionariness, forgetting the . . . conditions in which revolutionary methods are appropriate. . . ." ". . . genuine revolutionaries have most often broken their necks when they began to elevate 'revolution' to something almost divine, when they began to write 'revolution' with a capital R."

8. Whereas Leninist doctrine held that it could never be expedient to initiate highly destructive methods—such as force and extreme verbal attack—within the Bolshevik fraction (before 1912) or within the Party (after 1912), Stalinist doctrine holds that it frequently is expedient.

9. In deciding upon what statements to make both within the Party and without, the leadership must not be influenced by considerations of truth. Only the impact of these statements should be considered. Bourgeois governments are held to follow the same rule.

There are occasions when falsehoods—which are obvious to all informed groups—are useful.

In its May 4, 1948, letter to the Belgrade Politburo, the Moscow Politburo described this device (attributing it to the Yugoslavs):

> ...the Yugoslav leaders are using ... [the] method of complete denial of their errors regardless of their obvious existence ... the method of groundless denial of facts and documents....[13]

10. The Party leadership need not be concerned with consistency in its public statements. Again, only effectiveness is important.

11. Any political technique—from giving a reception to giving poison—must be regarded merely as a weapon in the Party's arsenal, to be used or not depending on the situation. However, *all* political techniques must constantly be kept in mind, and a decision to use (or not to use) any one of them must be based on the particular circumstances.

In the same way, the Party must be able quickly and easily to substitute one technique (e.g., violence) for another (e.g., legal measures).

12. The Party must be able to employ, simultaneously, techniques which "political philistines" would regard as incompatible (e.g., legal and illegal activities).

13. The Party must be "all-sided" in its activities: it must "take up positions in all spheres of the struggle without exception, put into proper shape all types of weapons . . . not neglecting in any way any one of them. . . . For nobody can say beforehand which sphere will serve as the first arena of battle. . . ."

14. "In a good household every rag comes in handy." That is, "any trifle should be utilized." Or, as an alternate image presents it: ". . . let us take the example of Gogol's Ossip who said: 'A small piece of string? Give it to me, even a small piece piece of string will be useful.' . . . We are not so rich in resources, not so strong that we can neglect a small piece of string." In any situation, with its specific opportunities, the

Party must ask itself: "Did we prove able to squeeze out of these opportunities all that could be squeezed out of them . . ." or are there "concealed reserves" which are being kept "idle"?

One "tactical principle of Leninism" is "the principle of the obligatory utilization . . . of even the smallest possibility of securing . . . even a temporary, vacillating, unstable, unreliable [ally]. . . ." "However weak and unimportant" any favorable change in the environment may be, "the party . . . must and will utilize it." Although some detail of the Party's policy may be "only a drop," still "we must not renounce any drop which hollows out the stone" of enemy policy. As "we do not know and cannot know which spark—out of the innumerable sparks that are flying around in all countries . . . will kindle the conflagration . . . we must . . . set to work to 'stir up' all, even the oldest, mustiest and seemingly hopeless spheres. . . ." That is: "the small things in a job should never be neglected, for it is from small things that the big thing is constructed."

15. The practices of capitalist society must be utilized: "We . . . have . . . such a powerful cause . . . that it can and *must* manifest itself in every form [ie., institution], both new and old; that it can . . . subjugate all forms, not only the new, but also the old—not for the purpose of reconciling itself with the old, but for the purpose of converting all and sundry forms, new and old, into a weapon for the victory of Communism. . . . It is our duty as Communists to master all forms."

* * *

In accordance with the insistence on expediency and lack of concern about consistency (pars. 3, 7, 9, and 10), the Politburo has shown, during the last 15 years, an ability to adopt intermittently, or even continuously, conservative practices and ideologies for public use, which had once been completely rejected (e.g., Great Russian nationalism). Although such changes are partly intended to create the belief that the Politburo has adopted new convictions, it is more likely that it has retained orthodoxy.

The Politburo shows great facility in changing its lines abruptly (par. 11): in being respectable and subversive at the same time (par. 12). This characteristic flexibility has continued to invalidate Western beliefs that Bolshevik changes in line (e.g., the "dissolution" of the Comintern) are definitive abandonments of previous positions.

The concern to make the most of any situation or instrumentality, no matter how minor (par. 14), indicates why the Politburo allocates energy and resources to institutions like the United Nations. Although it ascribes to them a very limited influence on the major course of history, it nevertheless believes that they must be utilized.

CHAPTER 4
THE CALCULUS OF THE GENERAL LINE

1. Every line of Bolshevik conduct is either prescribed or forbidden. It is prescribed if it will maximise the power of the Party. It is forbidden if it will not. There is little behavior that is merely tolerated, or recommended.

2. The Party must at all times have a "complete set" of "definite," "precise," "clear" positions on all matters: ". . . to the devil with all people with 'indeterminate views'. . . ." (This is to counteract the fear that the Party might become the victim of "confusion," which is felt by Bolsheviks to be a Russian propensity.)

The Party's position on any matter must always be elaborated in "concrete" fashion. Bolshevik doctrine combats the tendency "to avoid the study of concrete forms, conditions, tasks . . . by means of general phrases."

The Party's position on any matter must always, in a "practical," "business-like" fashion, indicate the correct course of action. Bolshevik doctrine urges "the transition from general considerations to the question of how to make the first and practical step." Against this, it requires that "every practical proposal shall be formulated in the most precise form possible."

3. Such a position can be reached by preparatory stages, each of which must show the characteristics mentioned in par. 2, above.

In 1922, Lenin said:

> . . . when I was in exile in Siberia . . . I was an underground lawyer, because, being summarily exiled, I was not allowed to practice; but as there were no other lawyers in the region, people came to me and told me about some of their affairs. But I had the greatest difficulty in understanding what it was all about. A woman would come to me and of course

13

start telling me all about her relatives and it would be incredibly difficult to get from her what she really wanted. Then she would tell me a story about a white cow. I would say to her: "Bring me a copy." She would then go off complaining: "He won't hear what I have to say about the white cow unless I bring a copy." We in our colony used to have a good laugh over this copy. But I was able to make some progress. People came to me, brought copies of the necessary documents, and I was able to gather what their trouble was, what they complained of, what ailed them."[14]

In 1921, Lenin wrote that "the Party is sick" (referring to the "discussion" within the Party on the "trade union question"). He went on:

What must be done to achieve the most rapid and surest cure? *All* members of the Party must with . . . greatest care *study* (1) the essence of the disagreements and (2) the development of the struggle within the Party. . . . we must unfailingly demand very exact, printed documents capable of being verified from all sides.[15]

Under Stalinism this point is applied, if at all, only to internal deliberations of policy-makers.

Thus, Bolshevik doctrine is opposed to proceeding by suggestions, explorations, thinking out loud, etc.

4. Although the Party leadership need not be concerned with the consistency of the *statements* it makes to the Party and to the rest of the world, it must be sure of the consistency of its *position* on all issues, in order to avoid the danger of accepting estimates of a situation and recommended courses of action which might be incompatible.

5. The Party must always be oriented to facts, present and future. It must guard against the danger of being "carried away by phrases," of being "deafened by words," of "replacing analysis by shouts," of permitting "the tongue to dominate thoughts."

6. The Party must arrive at every one of its policy decisions on the basis of an intensive and repeated process of calculation.

"We must act according to the rule, 'measure your cloth seven times before you cut' "; for every "task," it must be "precisely ascertained" which is the "correct approach" to it.

The Party should be as soberly deliberate in its calculations at the height of a "revolutionary crisis" as in a period of "relative stabilization of capitalism." Any carelessness in planning threatens catastrophe.

In 1920, Lenin said about the defeated Russian Socialist Revolutionary Party:

> . . . this Party . . . stubbornly refused to . . . understand the need for a strictly objective estimate of the class forces and their inter-relations before every political action.[16]

7. As every particular event and policy must be assessed in terms of its direct and indirect impact on the power of the Party, the Party must make all appraisals "on a sufficiently broad scale, that is, precisely on a world scale."

8. The bourgeois enemy, just like the Party, determines all the details of all its policies according to a central plan.

9. But the enemy may attempt to deceive the Party on this by alleging that certain of his policy details were due to oversights or mistakes. The Party must expose these deceptions.

10. Although the Party is not explicitly affirmed to be infallible, it is, in fact, believed to have a near-monopoly of correct estimates and forecasts: "Our strength lies in . . . the sober evaluation of *all* the existing class forces, Russian and international."

11. Although the predictive ability of the "bourgeoisie" is inferior to the Party's, it is superior to that of the "petty bourgeosie" (the small producers) and of the "masses."

12. The Party's activities must be determined on the basis of long-range forecasts.

In a November 1, 1926, speech at the Fifteenth Party Conference, Stalin entitled his sixth chapter: "The Decisive Importance of the Question of Perspectives of our Constructive Work." Alluding to a discussion on whether socialism in one country is possible, he said:

It may be asked: "Why all these disputes about the character and perspectives of our revolution, why these disputes about what is going to happen in the future or what is possible in the future—is it not better to cast aside all these disputes and to concern oneself with practical work?" I think, comrades, that such a question is utterly incorrect. We cannot move forward without knowing where it is necessary to go, without knowing the aims of the movement. We cannot build without perspectives. . . . Without clear perspectives, without clear aims, the Party cannot lead the work of construction. We cannot live according to the recipe of Bernstein: "The movement is everything, the aim nothing." We, in contrast, as revolutionaries, must subordinate . . . practical work to the basic . . . aim of proletarian construction.[17]

13. The Party must be able "to hear the grass grow beneath the soil," i.e., to make predictions which may seem absurd to "political philistines" but which will turn out to have been correct.

When forming policy, the Party must take into account not only the current relation of forces, but also future changes which may make the strong of today the weak of tomorrow, and vice versa.

In 1925, Stalin said:

The forces of the revolutionary movement in China are immeasurable. They have not yet come into anything like full operation. The future will show how vast they are. The rulers of the west and the east, who do not see these forces, who do not make sufficient allowance for their strength, will find out when the time comes. We, as a state, cannot but take such forces into account.[18]

In 1938, he wrote:

We must not base our orientation on the strata of society which are no longer developing, even though they at present constitute the predominant force, but on those strata which are developing and have a future before them, even though they at present do not constitute the predominant force. In the eighties of the past century, the proletariat in Russia constituted an insignificant minority of the population, whereas the ... peasants constituted the vast majority of the population. But the proletariat was developing as a class, whereas the peasantry as a class was disintegrating. And just because the proletariat was developing as a class the Marxists based their orientation on the proletariat. And they were not mistaken, for, as we know, the proletariat subsequently grew from an insignificant force into a first-rate historical and political force.[19]

14. The forecasts of the Party must be sober: ". . . revolutionaries will perish . . . only if . . . they lose their sobriety of outlook"; "Bolsheviks do not believe in miracles."

15. "We must formulate our programs in such a fashion that we are prepared for the worst; the occurrence of more favorable circumstances will only facilitate our work . . ."; "we must count on the worst."

In 1901, Lenin developed a plan for the organization of the Russian Social Democratic Labor Party in its fight against tsarism, and added:

We have spoken all the time about systematic ... preparation, but we have no desire ... to suggest that the autocracy may fall only as a result of a properly prepared siege or organized attack. . . . It is ... far more probable that the autocracy will fall under the pressure of one of those spontaneous outbursts or unforeseen political complications which constantly threaten it. . . . But no political party, if it desires to avoid adventurist tactics can base its activities on expectations of such outbursts and complications. . . . The less we count on the unexpected, the less likely are we to be taken by surprise by any "historical turn."[20]

16. The Party must not engage itself in either political or military operations with insufficient forces, hoping to make up the deficiency in the course of the operation. Violation of this rule is "adventurism."

17. At all times the Party must determine its policies with a

view to coming crises (which may be either favorable or unfavorable to the Party).

In 1925, Stalin said:

> We must utilize the period of quiet for ... rendering the party "always ready" for all possibilities of "complications." For "unknown is the day and the hour" when "the bridegroom cometh," opening the way to a new revolutionary surge.[21]

Discussing in 1925 the national question in Yugoslavia, Stalin said about the deviationist, Semich:

> A third error is his endeavor to deal with the national question in Yugoslavia as though it were quite unconnected with ... the probable course of events in Europe. Starting from the fact that at the present moment there is no serious movement for independence among the Croats and the Slovenes, Comrade Semich reaches the conclusion that the right of nations to constitute themselves into independent states is of academic interest only. . . . Even if we admit that, for the moment, the question has no actuality, yet, in the event of war breaking out, it would become very actual indeed. It would become equally actual if a revolution were to take place. . . . When in 1912, we Russian Marxists were drafting our first program concerning the national question, there was no serious movement for national independence in any region of the tsarist empire. Nevertheless we deemed it necessary to include in our program ... the right of every national minority to sever itself from the state to which it is attached. . . . Why did we do this? Because we based our program not merely upon events as they were then, but upon events which were in course of preparation; because we reckoned not only with the present, but likewise with the future.[22]

18. The enemy follows the same rule.

In 1919, Lenin said:

> ... the political leaders of the bourgeoisie have long understood the inevitability of civil war and are excellently, thoughtfully and systematically making preparations for it. . . .[23]

*   *   *

Soviet negotiators are averse to—or even seem to accept a tabu on—free exploration of problems with the other parties to the negotiation. They tend to present fully elaborated positions, keeping ready for substitution under certain circumstances other positions, which are put forward with the same finality (pars. 2 and 3).

When announcing decisions, the Politburo expresses itself to the world at large in the violent rhetoric of a Vishinsky, but in its internal deliberations it presumably maintains an attitude of great sobriety (pars. 5, 6, and 14).

The Politburo is always ready to use its position in one sphere of affairs as a means to advance—or to prevent retreat—in another. Thus, measures of retaliation may often be taken which seem to lack connection with the action against which they are directed (pars. 7 and 8).

The insight attributed to the bourgeosie proper (par. 11) helps to explain why the Politburo keeps a respectful eye on "Wall Street," while it regards its "progressive" "friends" abroad with contempt.

The belief that the Party should act on the basis of long-range forecasts (par. 12) helps to explain why the Politburo began to prepare for a future conflict with the West very soon after the direction of the German-Soviet war had begun to turn in 1943.

The Politburo presumably tends to feel today that its Chinese policy for the past 30 years proves its unique insight into political developments and its ability to determine current policies on the basis of accurate predictions (par. 13).

Consistent with the rules that evaluations of the future must be sober and take account of future crises (pars. 14 and 17), the Politburo feels that no great reliance can be placed on the temporary prominence in foreign governments of elements that are "friendly" to the Soviet Union.

CHAPTER 5
THE CONTROL OF FEELINGS

1. The Party line must be rationally calculated and must be distinguished from "moods," both within the Party and without, that might affect it.

In 1907, discussing the question of boycotting the election to the Third Duma, Lenin recalled the Menshevik rejection in 1905 of the boycott of the so-called Bulygin Duma proposed by the government.

> The Mensheviks were wrong not because they showed in this question a lack of a subjective revolutionary mood but because . . . [they] remained behind the objectively revolutionary situation. It is easy to confuse these two causes of the error of the Mensheviks, but it is inappropriate for a Marxist to do so.[24]

2. "Replacing objective analysis by 'feelings' "—to *any* extent —threatens catastrophe.

3. A Bolshevik must have perfect control over his feelings. All his political activity is "a most coldblooded . . . war."

Any imperfection in the Bolshevik's control over his feelings will cause him to become dominated by them. This will result in catastrophe.

4. These precepts hold true even when the feelings are in themselves laudable: a "revolutionary out of sentiment" is not a "real revolutionary."

In 1918, Lenin said about the Brest-Litovsk peace:

> It seems to me that the major reason for the disagreements among the Soviet parties on this question consists in this— that some permit themselves to be carried away too much by the feeling of legitimate and just indignation about the defeat which imperialism has inflicted on the Soviet power, and that they sometimes fall too much into despair . . . they

attempt to give to a question concerning the tactics of the revolution an answer which is based on immediate sentiment. . . . Instead of estimating . . : the task of the revolution . . . from the point of view of class forces, they demand that the most serious and most difficult questions be decided under the pressure of sentiments, only from the point of view of sentiments.[25]

5. The "spontaneity" of the masses leads to inexpedient behavior; hence the Party must not "yield" to it.

The Party must not yield to such "spontaneity" even when it runs in a "revolutionary" direction.

In 1920, Lenin affirmed that an anti-parliamentary mood was widespread among revolutionary workers in western Europe, and added:

But it would be not only unreasonable but actually criminal to yield to this mood. . . . In many countries of western Europe the revolutionary mood is at present, we might say, a "novelty," or a "rarity," for which we have been . . . waiting for a long time, and perhaps that is why we could easily give way to moods. Of course, without a revolutionary mood among the masses . . . revolutionary tactics will never be converted to action; but we in Russia have been convinced by long, painful and bloody experience of the truth that revolutionary tactics cannot be built up on revolutionary moods alone.[26]

6. The Party must be able to undertake policies which will expediently simulate friendliness toward, and may bestow advantages on, outsiders actually regarded with intense hostility.

In the summer of 1918, Lenin recalled the negotiations with the Allies early that year:

When in February 1918, the . . . [Germans] led their troops against . . . demobilized Russia . . . I did not hesitate in the least to enter into a "compromise" with French monarchists. Captain Sadoul of the French Army, who sympathized with the Bolsheviks in words but in deeds faithfully served French imperialism, brought a French officer, de Lubersac, to see me. I am a monarchist, my sole object is to secure the defeat of Germany, he said. *Cela va sans dire,* I replied.

This did not in the least prevent me from "compromising" with de Lubersac concerning the service which French officers, expert sappers, desired to render us in blowing up railway tracks to hinder the advance of the Germans. . . . The French monarchist and I shook hands, knowing that each of us would willingly have hanged his "partner." For a time, however, our interests coincided.[27]

In 1920, Lenin said, pointing to the intensification of inter-enemy conflicts which resulted from the Soviet policy of offering economic "concessions":

. . . that is why . . . we must with all our heart—or better, without a heart, but calculatingly—favor concessions.[28]

7. A Bolshevik must not feel insulted by any kind of behavior that outsiders may show toward him, although it may be expedient to simulate such feelings.

8. A Bolshevik must not act out of feelings of offense.

In 1933, Stalin urged collective farms to accept independent farmers who had hitherto been hostile to them. He commented:

Of course, we must understand the attitude of the collective farmers. . . . During the past years they have often been the butt of insults and sneers on the part of the individual farmers. But we must not attach the slightest importance to these insults and sneers. He is a bad leader who cannot forget an offense, and who puts his own feelings above the interest of the . . . cause. If you want to be leaders, you must be able to forget the insults to which you were subjected. . . . Two years ago I received a letter from a peasant woman, a widow, living in the Volga region. She complained that the collective farm refused to accept her as a member, and she demanded my support. I made inquiries at the collective farm. I received a reply . . . stating that they could not accept her because she had insulted a collective farm meeting. . . . It seems that at a meeting of peasants at which the collective farmers called upon the individual farmers to join the collective farm, this very widow in reply to this appeal had lifted up her skirt and said—"Here, take your collective farm!" . . . Could her application to join the collective farm be rejected if, a year later, she sincerely repented and admitted her error? I think that her application should not be rejected, and that is what I wrote to the collective farm. The widow was accepted into the collective farm. . . . It turns out that she is now working in the front ranks. This, then, is another example which shows that leaders, if they want to remain leaders, must be able to forget an offense if the interests of the cause demand it.[29]

The Party must be able to delay punitive measures until the most useful moment.

9. The Party must not "succumb to panic." In particular, the Party must not permit itself to be "frightened" by "terrible words" that exaggerate the unfavorable aspects of a situation.

*　　　*　　　*

Considering other governments to be motivated by principles similar to their own, the Politburo does not believe that foreign leaders are influenced to any extent by sentiments when forming policy, and would despise them if they were.

Concern over the dangers likely to arise when feelings, even laudable ones, interfere with the objective analysis of events, as well as the belief that the masses are particularly susceptible to such behavior (pars. 2 through 5), leads the Politburo to stress that in the complicated transition from capitalism to communism expedient policies are often uncongenial to the masses and distasteful to leaders who have not learned to discipline their feeling.

During 1941–1944, the Politburo behaved toward its allies in accordance with par. 6—simulating good will toward outsiders whom they actually regarded with intense hostility.

Consistent with par. 6, as also with its tendency to view others in its own image, the Politburo suspects the genuineness of the good feelings of its allies for the Soviet Union.

It is compatible with the rules that a Bolshevik should not feel offense at any behavior of outsiders toward him, or act on the basis of such feelings (pars. 7 and 8), that in situations falling short of severe crisis the Politburo may simulate feelings (or give free rein to real feelings) of offense as a device of resistance to encroachment upon its domain.

During the period, beginning in 1945, of its severe military inferiority to the United States, the behavior of the Politburo has been consistent with the belief that the Party must not be frightened by unfavorable situations (par. 9).

CHAPTER 6
EFFECTIVE ACTION

1. Any tendency toward passivity must be opposed. The Party must not take the course of least resistance. There are always some elements in the Party that "wish to swim with the stream, smoothly and calmly."

In 1930, Stalin said:

> In our Party there are some who think that we ought not to have called a halt to the Left exaggerators [of collectivization rates]. They think that we ought not to have offended our workers and counteracted their excitement, even if this excitement led to mistakes. . . . Only those who want at all costs to swim with the stream can say that. They are the very same people who will never learn the Leninist policy of going against the stream when . . . the interests of the Party demand it. They are tailists and not Leninists.[30]

2. Every activity of the Party involves "fighting" and "overcoming difficulties."

3. The Party must always exert its full strength when in action; it must avoid both inactivity and exhaustion. ". . . a most irreconcilable struggle must be carried on against all defence of sluggishness." The Party must perform its work "with clenched teeth," "with enormous exertion," "exerting all its forces and not being halted by any sacrifice."

Thus, even when applying "the tactics of defence," "the Party . . . must keep the enemy in a state of constant exertion." If the Party decides to avoid battle for the time being, "this does not mean that the Party should merely wait, folding its arms, transforming itself into a sterile bystander. . . ."

4. The Party's activities must proceed "without respite," "incessantly," "continuously."

5. Favorable developments occur only as a consequence of

strenuous and unremitting effort: "nothing [good] ever comes of itself."

In 1930, Stalin surveyed recent economic gains of the regime:

> It would be a mistake to think that we have secured these achievements "easily and quietly," automatically, so to speak, without special efforts and strain of will, without struggle and disturbance. Such achievements do not come automatically. ... We have won these achievements by ... serious and prolonged struggle to overcome the difficulties.[31]

In 1931, Stalin said:

> There are ... executives who ... think ... that the shortage of labor will disappear of its own accord, so to speak. This is a delusion, comrades. The difficulties in the supply of labor power cannot disappear of themselves. They will disappear only as a result of our own efforts.[32]

6. Major advances do not justify a relaxation of effort; catastrophe may, at any time, result from a relaxation of effort.

In 1933, Stalin said:

> Many think that once we have achieved, say, seventy or eighty per cent of collectivization in a given district or in a given region we have got all we need, and can then let things take their natural course, let things go their own way, on the assumption that collectivization will do its work itself and will raise agriculture to a higher level. But this is a profound delusion, comrades. As a matter of fact, the transition to collective farming as a predominant form of farming does not diminish but increases our cares in regard to agriculture. ... Letting things take their own course is now more dangerous than ever for the development of agriculture. Letting things take their own course may prove fatal to the whole cause.[33]

7. Expending too much effort on carrying out a policy is a smaller mistake than expending too little effort.

In 1907, Lenin recalled his concentration, in 1900–

1902, on the problems of the organization of the Party:

> To say at the present moment that *Iskra* exaggerated (*in the years 1901–1902!*) the idea of an organization of professional revolutionaries is equivalent to reproaching the Japanese *after* the Russian-Japanese War for an exaggeration of Russian military power before the war, for exaggerated concern with the struggle against this power. The Japanese had to strain all efforts against a possible maximum of Russian forces in order to be victorious. . . . *Today* the idea of an organization of professional revolutionaries has . . . achieved complete victory. This victory would have been impossible if one had not put, at the time, this idea into the *foreground,* if one had not preached it in an "exaggerated" fashion to those who were obstacles to its realization.[34]

8. Any imperfect performance threatens catastrophe: "It is . . . necessary to consider all one's smallest mistakes, and then we will win. . . ." ". . . exaggeration of a line, even in the slightest degree, means preventing victory."

9. A Bolshevik must concentrate on major tasks in order to prevent a dissipation of effort. "The main thing is not to disperse one's energy."

10. ". . . the whole of political life is an endless chain consisting of an infinite number of links. The whole art of politics lies in finding the link that can be least torn out of our hands, the one that is most important at the given moment, the one that guarantees the command of the whole chain, and having found it, to cling to that link as tightly as possible." That is, "it is not sufficient to be . . . a Communist in general. One must be able at each particular moment to find that special link. . . ." "We have understood how to be victorious because we ascertained correctly what the most urgent . . . task was, and because we concentrated all forces . . . on this task."

In 1937, Stalin said:

> . . . whilst the wreckers of the Shakhti period deceived our people in technique, taking advantage of the technical backwardness of the latter, the contemporary wreckers, possess-

ing Party membership cards, deceive our people's political confidence in them ... taking advantage of the political unconcern of our people.

It is necessary to supplement the old slogan of mastering technique, corresponding with the period of the Shakhti days, by a new slogan ... the abolition of our political credulity, that is, by a slogan ... in accordance with the period through which we are now passing.

It may be asked: Was it ... not possible ... in the days of the Shakhti period to have proclaimed both slogans at once...? No, it was not possible. Things are not done in that way in the Bolshevik Party.... Some one main slogan as the central one is always brought forward so that in grasping it the whole chain may be pulled along. Lenin thus taught us: Find the main link in the chain of our work, pull it so that the whole chain is drawn along, and thus go forward.[35]

11. ". . . . we must invent not pious wishes but practical, hard 'first steps'." What is required at any given moment is "a modest taking into account of the probable and possible next conquest, instead of an 'untactical' . . . claim to win total victory." "The most important task" is that of "fighting the danger of being carried away by vast plans and tasks."

In March, 1918, Lenin said:

I leave it to others to dream about international revolution. ... Everything will come in due time; for the time being, set to work to create self-discipline, obey ... so that the workers may learn to fight for at least one hour in twenty-four. This is much more difficult than writing beautiful fairy tales. This is the position today; by that you will help the German revolution, the international revolution.[36]

12. A Bolshevik must oppose what is regarded as a traditional Russian tendency to dwell on the level of feeling, thought, and words rather than to proceed to action.

In particular the objection is to "the inclination to substitute discussions for action, talk for work." "A correct political line is not needed as a declaration, but as something to be carried into effect."

In 1934, Stalin described a "type of executive" who "retards our work, hinders our work, and holds up our advance":

I have in mind the . . . honest windbags . . . who are . . . incapable of organizing anything. Last year I had a conversation with one such comrade, a very respected comrade, but an incorrigible windbag, capable of drowning any living cause in a flood of talk. Here is the conversation. I: How are you getting on with the sowing? He: With the sowing, Comrade Stalin? We have mobilized ourselves. I: Well, and what then? He: We have put the question squarely. I: And what next? He: There is a turn, Comrade Stalin; soon there will be a turn. I: But still? He: We can say that there is an indication of some progress. I: But for all that, how are you getting on with the sowing? He: So far, Comrade Stalin, we have not made any headway with the sowing. . . . A Ukranian worker recently described the state of a certain organization when he was asked whether that organization had any definite line: "Well," he said, "they have a line all right, but they don't seem to be doing any work."[37]

Against this, the Bolshevik demands economy in words.

13. "Waving one's arms about in public," that is, "the use of mere gestures in an attempt to be impressive," is opposed. Stalin said, in 1926:

A policy of gesticulation has been the characteristic feature of the policy of Trotsky since the time he came to the Party. The first application of this policy we had at the time of the Brest peace, when Trotsky did not sign the German-Russian peace and gesticulated, in an attempt to be impressive, against the peace treaty, assuming that the proletariat of all countries could be made to rise against imperialism by gesticulation.[38]

14. Similarly, the temptation to believe in the automatic effectiveness of verbal aggression must be resisted.

In 1920, Lenin said about the anti-parliamentarism of

"Left Communists" in Europe:

> ... the "Lefts" ... mistake the subjective "rejection" of a
> certain reactionary institution for its actual destruction. ...
> To express one's "revolutionariness" solely by ... repudi-
> ating participation in parliaments is very easy.[39]

In 1931, Stalin said:

> I know a number of business executives who in their fight
> against lack of personal responsibility confine themselves
> to speaking at meetings now and then, hurling curses at the
> lack of personal responsibility, evidently in the belief that
> after such speeches lack of personal responsibility will
> disappear. ...[40]

15. There is apprehension about Party members showing a
"reversion to the old slackness of will" of Russians.

The Party must combine "the wide outlook of the Russian
revolutionist" with "American practicality." [Stalin, 1924]

"American practicality is that . . . spirit . . . that simply
must go through with a job, once it has been tackled, even if it
be of minor importance." Bolshevik doctrine combats the "general weakness" that "may be connected with the Slavic character,
with the fact that . . . we persevere insufficiently to the end
in the pursuit of a given aim."

*   *   *

The rejection of passivity and the insistence on continuous
exertion of the Party's full strength (pars. 1 through 4) enjoin
the Politburo not to limit its expansion to what it can "comfort-
ably chew" but to go to the limit of what seems at all practicable.

The belief that favorable developments result from unremitting effort and that advances do not justify relaxation of such
efforts (pars. 5 and 6) tend to indicate that a reduction in
international tension is unlikely unless the Politburo should
come to believe that further pressure by it might "provoke" an
undesired showdown.

Consistent with par. 11, the Politburo has, since 1945, always
concentrated on specific and limited objectives, pursuing them
with much energy.

CHAPTER 7

PERSEVERANCE AND FLEXIBILITY

1. "There is no such thing as an absolutely inextricable position." Through perseverance, effective action can be carried out even under the most difficult conditions.

2. A Bolshevik must persevere to the end of any action, no matter how unpleasant.

In 1916, Lenin wrote to a member of the editorial board of *The Communist* (published in Switzerland):

> You write that you "are sick and tired of ... correspondence and negotiations ..." I understand you completely, but you must be patient! Once you have gone into the business of negotiating, it is impermissible to get nervous and fall into despair. That would not be proletarian, now, would it?[41]

3. "A mass without a Party . . . is incapable of perseverance."

The emotions of the "masses" and of the "intelligentsia" are "unstable"; those of Bolsheviks should be stable.

4. A Bolshevik must oppose "vacillation" ("inability to maintain a definite political line," "lack of steadiness in matters of principle," "hysterical rushing from place to place"). He must also oppose lack of continuity ("incapacity for sustained effort," doing things "spasmodically" rather than "systematically").

In 1921, Lenin said:

> ... hard conditions of life give rise to vacillation for the bourgeoisie today, for the proletariat tomorrow. The hardened proletarian vanguard alone is capable of withstanding and overcoming vacillation.[42]

In 1927, Stalin described the development of opposition attitudes toward the Anglo-Russian trade-union

31

committee:

> First the opposition was enchanted with the Anglo-Russian Committee. The opposition even affirmed that the Anglo-Russian Committee is a means "to render harmless" reformism in Europe (Zinoviev).... Second, when the opposition finally recognized that Purcell [the British trade-union leader] and his friends are reformists, it passed from enchantment to disenchantment, more than that—to despair, and demanded immediate rupture as a means to overthrow the Trade Union Council....[43]

5. On the other hand, the Party must know how to adapt itself to all changes in its environment: ". . . it is our duty as Communists . . . to adapt our tactics to every change that is called forth by something other than our class, or our efforts."

In 1905, Lenin said about the agrarian policy of the Party:

> The decisive point is that the conduct of the revolutionary proletariat towards the conflict between peasants and landowners cannot be the same in all cases and under all conditions of the various phases of the Russian revolution. Under certain conditions . . . this conduct must be not only one of sympathy, but of direct support, and not only one of support, but of "incitement." Under other circumstances, this conduct can and must be a neutral one. . . . It is not only our "Socialist Revolutionaries" who are full of the vulgar illusions of revolutionary democracy, but many Social Democrats who . . . look for a "simple" solution of the task, one which would be the same for all combinations.[44]

There must be no "doctrinaire attitude . . . against changes in strategy and tactics. . . ."

Flexibility is necessary to avoid catastrophe and to ensure victory.

In 1925, Stalin said:

> Certain Party members maintain that since we have the New Economic Policy . . . our task should be to carry on unbendingly . . . until a general smash-up occurs. . . . What we need now is not to carry on unbendingly, but to show a

maximum of elasticity. . . . In the absence of such elasticity we shall not be able . . . to keep our place at the helm. We need the utmost elasticity in order to keep the Party at the helm. . . .[45]

The Party must never tie its hands in advance, that is, never restrict its "freedom in the choice of political means."

In March, 1918, Lenin said, rejecting a proposal by Trotsky to modify a resolution on war and peace:

We must in no case, in not even a single strategic maneuver, tie our own hands. . . . We must say that the Party Congress commissions the Central Committee to denounce all peace treaties and to declare war on every imperialist state and on the whole world as soon as the Central Committee of the Party regards the moment as appropriate. We must give the Central Committee the power to denounce the Brest-Litovsk Peace at any moment. But this does not mean that we shall denounce it immediately in the present situation. . . . We must in no case limit our Central Party body, neither with reference to the denunciation of the peace treaty, nor with reference to the declaration of a war. . . . We must not tie our hands by a resolution that we shall sign no peace treaty. . . . The peace treaty is merely a piece of live maneuvering. Either we stand on this viewpoint of maneuvering or we formally bind our hands in advance in such a fashion that we shall not be able to move.[46]

The Party "must not blindly worship the particular phase in which it may find itself at any particular time or place"; it must be ready to change its strategy, tactics, organization as changed conditions require it, without being hindered by "the prejudices and memories of what was yesterday."

6. Therefore, "If I pursue an enemy who does not move in a straight line but zigzags, then I too must zigzag in order to reach him."

7. When "the turns of history are very sharp," the turns of the Party's policy may also have to be sharp.

8. The Party must adapt itself to changes which follow from its own policies, and which could not have been foreseen.

In 1930, Stalin discussed the work of the Central Committee during the years 1928–1930 when the Committee "corrected and perfected the Five Year Plan to increase the rate of progress and to shorten the periods." He commented:

It may be said that by changing the estimates of the Five Year Plan so fundamentally, the Central Committee infringes the principle of planning. But ... for us Bolsheviks ... the Five Year Plan, like every plan, is only a scheme adopted as a first approach which has to be ... altered ... on the basis of the experience of its fulfillment. ... Only bureaucrats can imagine that the work of planning is *concluded* with the compilation of a plan. The compilation of a plan is only the *beginning of planning*. Real planned guidance develops only ... in the course of its [the plan's] application, by correcting it ... rendering it more exact.[47]

9. The Party should, during every non-critical period, be as prepared for the indefinite continuation of "calm" as for a sudden development permitting it to advance, or the enemy to attack.

In 1902, Lenin said:

... unless we are able to devise political tactics, and an organizational plan based precisely upon calculations for *work over a long period of time,* and at the same time, *in the very process of this work,* put our party into readiness to spring to its post ... at the very first, even unexpected, call, as soon as the progress of events becomes accelerated, we will prove to be but miserable political adventurers. ... It would be a grievous error indeed to build up the party organization in the expectation only of outbreaks of street-fighting, or only upon the "forward march of the drab, everyday struggle." We must *always* carry on our everyday work and always be prepared for everything, for very frequently it is almost impossible to foresee beforehand when periods of outbreaks will give away to periods of calm. And even in those cases when it is possible to do so, it will not be possible to utilize this foresight for the purpose of reconstructing our organization, because ... these changes from turmoil to calm take place with astonishing rapidity. ...[48]

10. The Party must not regard the existence of either "close relations" or of "rupture of relations" with an outside group as definitive for any length of time.

11. It is irrelevant that, in the eyes of "political philistines," an expedient policy of flexibility results in "inconsistent" courses of action.

In 1919, Lenin said:

> We shall be called upon to make very frequent changes in our line of conduct which to the casual observer may appear strange and incomprehensible. "How is that?" he will say. "Yesterday you were making promises to the petty bourgeoisie, while today Dzerzhinsky announces that the Left Socialist Revolutionaries and the Mensheviks will be placed against the wall. What an inconsistency!"[49]

12. To achieve the greatest degree of flexibility, the Party must be "monolithic" in its internal structure.

In 1923, Stalin said:

> ... the unexampled unity and compactness of our Party ... made it possible to avoid a split on the occasion of a turn as sharp as that of the NEP [New Economic Policy]. Not a single party in the world ... would have withstood such a sharp turn without confusion, without a split. ... As is well known, such turns are apt to lead to the falling by the wayside of a certain group. ... We have had such a turn in the history of our Party in 1907 and 1908 ... two whole groups then fell from our cart.[50]

*　　*　　*

The coexistence of the rules enjoining perseverance (pars. 1 and 4), on the one hand, and flexibility (pars. 5 and 8), on the other, explains why Politburo policy often gives an impression of being both rigid and elastic.

The rapprochements of the Politburo to outside groups, as well as the severance of relations with them (unless the time for their liquidation has come), are not regarded as definitive, regardless of propaganda to the contrary (par. 10).

Consistent with its lack of concern about "philistine" conceptions of consistency (par. 11), the Politburo never regards itself as committed today to a line taken yesterday, as was shown, for instance, in the developments of its German policy after 1945.

CHAPTER 8
ORGANIZATION

1. A high degree of organization is a necessary condition for success in any political enterprise.

Lenin said in 1902:

> I used to work in a circle that set itself a great ... task: and every member of that circle suffered to the point of torture from the realization that we were proving ourselves to be amateurs at a moment in history when we might have been able to say ... : "Give us an organization of revolutionists and we shall overturn the whole of Russia!"[51]

Stalin said in 1934:

> In order to overcome ... difficulties and achieve success, it was necessary to *organize* the struggle. ...[52]

2. A Bolshevik must oppose "Russian lack of organization." "Organized activity was never a strong point with the Russians in general, nor with the Bolsheviks in particular." [Lenin, 1919]

3. "The great whole which we are creating for the first time—the Party" [Lenin, 1904] makes of Party members "people of a special mold." [Stalin, 1935]

4. The Party is the only perfect organization that exists.

In 1924, Stalin spoke about the recent entry of 200,000 workers into the Party:

> Our Party has become the elected organ of the working class. Show me another party like that. You won't be able to show it, as another such party does not yet exist in nature. Curiously enough, even such a powerful party doesn't please our oppositionists. Where then will they find a better party on earth? I am afraid that they will have to jump over to Mars in their search for a better party.[53]

5. The Party must oppose "diffuse," "loose" forms of Party organization in favor of "strict," "tight" forms.

6. The Party must be "monolithic"; that is, it is essential to have unanimity within the Party. Any lack of unanimity would result in the fragmentation of the Party.

In a speech to the Tenth Party Congress in 1921, when "fractions" inside the Party were outlawed, Lenin referred to:

> ... the extraordinary richness of platforms, shades, shades of shades ... that have been formulated and discussed. . . .[54]

7. Bolshevism is also opposed to what it regards as a Russian tendency toward dispersion of power.

In his 1946 election speech, Stalin said about the Soviet Union at large:

> As you know, prominent foreign pressmen have more than once gone on record to the effect that the Soviet multi-national state was an "artificial," "non-viable structure," that in the event of any complications ... the fate of Austria-Hungary awaited the Soviet Union. . . . These gentlemen did not understand that the parallel with Austria-Hungary did not apply. . . .[55]

8. All effective political action stems from a select leadership. ". . . without the 'dozen' of tried and talented leaders . . . no class in modern society is capable of conducting a determined struggle." [Lenin, 1902]

In 1919, Lenin said:

> The stratum of workers who actually administered Russia during this year, who carried out the whole policy and who constituted our strength—this stratum in Russia is an incredibly thin one. . . . If a future historian ever comes to collect information regarding the groups which administered Russia during these seventeen months, how many hundreds or how many thousands of individuals were engaged in this work and bore the whole incredible burden of administering the country—nobody will believe that this could have been accomplished by such an insignificant number of individuals.[56]

In 1934, in an interview with H. G. Wells, who said:
"I wander around the world as a common man and,
as a common man, observe what is going on around
me," Stalin answered:

> Important public men like yourself are not "common." Of
> course, history alone can show how important this or that
> public man has been; at all events, you do not look at the
> world as a "common man."[57]

9. A structure and degree of centralization similar to that
existing in the Party are attributed to outside groups as well.

In his 1927 interview with the first American labor
delegation to Russia, Stalin answered their question of
"Is it correct to say that the Communist Party controls
the Russian government?" as follows:

> It is well known that the bourgeois parties in capitalist
> countries ... guide the government, and, moreover, that in
> these countries this guidance is concentrated in the hands
> of a narrow circle of individuals connected in one way or
> another with the big banks. ... Who does not know that
> every bourgeois party in England, or in other capitalist
> countries, has its secret cabinet consisting of a closed circle
> of persons who concentrate the guidance in their hands?[58]

* * *

In accordance with pars. 3 through 5, on the perfection of the
Party as an organization and the special qualities of its members, the Moscow leadership of the Communist Parties abroad
has been maintained despite the dissolution of the Comintern.
The continuity of a Communist Party would be equally un-
affected by an ostensible disappearance, for instance, behind a
National Front, as has been the case in recent years in Yugoslavia and Indo-China.

Again viewing others in its own image, the Politburo is apt
to exaggerate the power of "Wall Street" in the United States,
and the power of the United States in the noncommunist sector
of the world (par. 9).

CHAPTER 9
THE DANGER OF DEPENDENCY

1. The Party must never "put reliance" on support given by outside groups.

In 1925, Stalin discussed the reactions of the peasants to the agricultural policy of the regime:

> ... among the poor peasants ... it seemed that the abandonment of the attempt to make an end of the kulaks ... signified that the workers were ceasing to fight on behalf of the poor peasants. ... Thereupon, the poor peasants, instead of carrying on their own ... struggle against the kulaks, began to whine in the most shameful manner. The poor peasants are ... dominated by the ideology of state pensioners. They put their trust in the GPU, in the authorities, in anything you please except themselves. They cannot make up their minds to put their own shoulders to the wheel.[59]

2. However, the Party must try to "utilize" even the most unreliable sources of support: "Only those who have no reliance in themselves can fear to enter into temporary alliances with unreliable people."

*   *   *

These attitudes explain why communists give the impression, on the one hand, of putting the main emphasis on the Party, and, on the other hand, of being mainly preoccupied with infiltrating all accessible places outside of the Party.

CHAPTER 10
THE DANGER OF BEING "USED"

1. If the Party enters into any other relation than that of overt conflict with an outside group, it must "use" that group —or itself be "used" by it.

2. It is incumbent on the Party to defeat all attempts to "make use" of it.

> In 1939, Stalin said that "a task of the Party in the sphere of foreign policy" was:

> ... not [to] allow our country to be drawn into conflicts by warmongers who are accustomed to have others pull the chestnuts out of the fire for them.[60]

3. Failure to prevent this will result in loss of power and will bring degradation.

> In 1927, Stalin wrote that "the British bourgeoisie does not like to wage war with its own hands," and added:

> Sometimes it really succeeded in finding fools ready to pull its chestnuts out of the fire.[61]

4. To permit the Party to be "used" by an outside group would threaten annihilation, as it would ultimately be "thrown away like a dirty rag." Although the Party might not be aware of doing so, it would "cringe," "capitulate," "yield to pressure," "become subservient," "bow down," "be dragged in the wake" of the outsider, and "become his appendage," "puppet," "tail," "parrot"; it would "dance to the tune" of the master.

5. Anybody or anything near or inside the Party may become an enemy "tool." In order to prevent the enemy from striking at the Party with such a tool, the Party must never relax its vigilance, not even in situations that are apparently most reliable.

41

In 1933, Stalin said.

> From the point of view of Leninism, collective farms, like the Soviets . . . are a weapon and a weapon only. Under certain conditions, this weapon may be turned against the revolution. It can be turned against counter-revolution. It can serve the working class and the peasants. Under certain conditions it can serve the enemies of the working class and of the peasantry. It all depends upon who wields this weapon, and against whom it is directed.[62]

6. The Party must not permit itself to be persuaded by outsiders to change its position.

7. Nor must the Party "yield" to the "provocations" of an enemy.

> In 1918, Lenin stated that certain parts of the foreign bourgeoisie were attempting to "provoke the Russian Soviet republic into a clearly disadvantageous war," and called the "Left Communists" who were in favor of such a war: ". . . tools of imperialist provocation."

In 1928, Stalin wrote:

> The opposition makes a lot of noise protesting that they . . . invented the slogan of self-criticism, that the Party stole the slogan from them and thereby capitulated to the opposition. By acting in this way, the opposition is trying . . . to catch certain simpletons and to induce them to dissociate themselves from the Party slogan of self-criticism. And how do some of our comrades react to this? Instead of tearing the mask from the opposition's fraud and fighting for the slogan of Bolshevik self-criticism, they fall into the trap, dissociate themselves from the slogan of self-criticism, dance to the tune of the opposition, and capitulate to it, mistakenly believing that they are dissociating themselves from the opposition. . . . But in our work we cannot dance to anybody's tune. Still less can we allow ourselves to be guided in our work by what the members of the opposition say about us. We must pursue our own path, brushing aside both the fraudulent attempts of the opposition and the errors of

certain of our Bolsheviks who have fallen victims to the provocation of the opposition.[63]

Thus, Bolshevik doctrine holds that the reaction of the Party to an enemy act must not be predetermined by that act. For example, the Party must not feel that retaliation in kind is the only appropriate response to an offense. To believe this would mean to lose freedom of action and thus to "disarm" in the face of the enemy.

*   *   *

It has often been observed that the Politburo seems more apprehensive about initiating or tolerating contacts between the Soviet Union and the rest of the world than are Western governments. Some of the dangers which the Politburo perceives in contacts with the outer world are indicated in the points concerning the need to prevent outside groups from "using" the Party (pars. 1 through 6).

According to the rule against yielding to the provocations of an enemy (par. 7), the Politburo would not necessarily retaliate to a political offensive against the Soviet Union with war, unless it was convinced that the offensive carried a certain indication of imminent attack.

CHAPTER 11
ISOLATION AND CONTACT

1. Bolshevik doctrine opposes any "blurring" of the "boundaries" between the Party and the "masses." The line of demarcation between the Party and the class [the proletariat] must never be obliterated. If it should be, the Party sooner or later would cease to exist: it would "merge with" the masses, be "submerged within" them, "dissolve into" them.

2. On the other hand, the Party must not "shut itself up in its shell," "wall itself off" from the masses, or "cut itself off" from them, "degenerating into a closed circle." Such isolation would cause the Party sooner or later to succumb to its enemies: "The officer cadres of an army who become cut off from their army . . . are no more officer cadres."

3. One of the most important reasons for the Party to maintain contact with the masses is to keep informed of their attitudes and thus be better able to formulate practicable policies.

In 1923, Stalin said:

> There are two ways of governing a country. One . . . way is to have a simplified apparatus, headed by a group of people, or by a single person, having hands and eyes in the locality in the shape of governors. This is a very simple form of government, under which the ruler . . . receives the kind of information governors can supply. . . . Friction arises, friction passes into conflict, and conflict into revolt. The revolt is then crushed. This is not our system of government; besides, although simple, it is too costly. In our Soviet country we must evolve a system of government which will permit us, with certainty, to anticipate all changes, to perceive everything that is going on among the peasants, the non-Russian nations, and the Russians; the system of supreme organs must possess a number of barometers which will anticipate

44

every change, register and forestall a . . . bandit movement, a
Kronstadt, and all possible storms and ill-fortune. This is
the Soviet system of government. It is called the Soviet government, the People's government, because, being based on
the rank and file, it is first to register changes, to take
necessary measures. . . .[64]

4. The demarcation line between the Party and an area controlled by it, on the one hand, and any outside organizations,
on the other, must be as clear as that between the Party and
the masses and also be impossible to cross without the Party's
consent.

5. Once the Party has created sufficiently strong boundaries
between itself and its environment, it may enter into any expedient relation with any outside group.

In 1902, Lenin said about the Russian Social Democratic Labor Party:

It is absolutely required *first* to demarcate oneself from all,
and only to separate the proletariat, solely, uniquely, and
exclusively. Only *afterwards* must we declare that the proletariat will liberate everybody, that it calls to everybody,
appeals to everybody.[65]

6. Any degree of infiltration of "alien" elements into the
Party threatens catastrophe unless eliminated.

7. The unorganized elements around the Party (e.g., in
earlier phases of the Soviet regime—the "petty bourgeoisie,"
particularly in the countryside; in the present phase—"the sur-
vivals of capitalism in the minds of people") constantly tend to
seep into the Party.

The organized elements around the Party (e.g., foreign governments) constantly attempt to send agents into the Party.

Incessant and all-seeing vigilance are essential if mistakes
which might "open a path" into the Party for enemies are to
be avoided. Not only must no "door" be "open" to them,
but there must not be the smallest "crack" through which
some "worm" could "creep." There must be the closest in-
spection of the border (in the physical as well as the figurative

sense) to prevent "camouflaged contraband" from being "smuggled in."

8. When the Party is in alliance with other groups in a fight against a common enemy, it must conduct activities "parallel" to those of its allies; but it must not have closer relations with them because this would result in the Party's being "penetrated" by their intelligence and subversive agents.

*   *   *

Consistent with the rule concerning the necessity for clearly marked dividing lines between the Party and outside organizations (par. 4), the Politburo insisted on creating clear demarcation lines of power between itself and its allies in those areas of Europe and Asia where the Western powers desired collaboration in the early period after the second war. The creation of such demarcation lines was, for the Politburo, the precondition to collaboration with the powers across these lines (par. 5).

The rules concerning the dangers of infiltration (pars. 6 through 8) explain why the Politburo has always conducted an "iron curtain" policy.

CHAPTER 12
DECEPTION

1. Bolshevik doctrine stresses the use of deception as an enemy device and the danger of not perceiving this.

In 1926, Stalin stated:

> Lenin often said that it is difficult to take revolutionaries by the use of a rough fist, but that sometimes it is very easy to take them by kindness. We must never forget this truth. . . .[66]

Hence, a high degree of political insight includes a high degree of suspiciousness (i.e., the absence of "philistine trustfulness").

In 1926, Stalin said:

> To deceive our party is not such an easy matter.[67]

2. "The slogan of the Marxist workers is not to believe in words, but to check them most thoroughly. . . . Only fools believe in mere words."

Hence, in any dealings with outside groups, "we will wait for their *deeds*. We do not believe in promises."

3. An enemy may attempt to deceive by presenting himself as friendly toward the Party.

In 1938, Stalin said, in referring to criticisms of Marxism made by certain Bolsheviks 30 years earlier: ‚

> This criticism differs from the usual criticism in that it was not conducted openly and squarely, but in a veiled and hypocritical form under the guise of "defending" . . . Marxism. These people . . . hypocritically denied their hostility to Marxism and two-facedly continued to style themselves Marxists. . . . The more hypocritical grew this criticism . . . the more dangerous it was to the party. . . .[68]

4. All public statements made by outside groups are regarded as aiming to deceive. The few that are accepted at face value

(e.g., statements of aggressive intent toward the Soviet Union) are those which are apt to be termed "unprecedentedly cynical."

5. The "masses" tend to be easily deceived; hence, to correct their tendency to follow disastrous courses of action, the Party must "tear the mask from the face of the enemy."

6. One (Leninist) trend in Bolshevik doctrine is skeptical about the results which the Party can achieve by deception. In 1921, Lenin said:

> In our midst those who by politics mean petty devices which sometimes are almost on a par with deception should be very strongly condemned. . . . Classes cannot be deceived.[69]

7. Lenin implied that attempts to deceive the enemy might boomerang through their effect on the "masses" and must therefore be undertaken warily. Stalin implies that such repercussions can be taken in stride.

8. Lenin implied that the Party can take in its stride any unfavorable repercussions in the enemy camp resulting from a frank statement of policy to the masses and to the Party; Stalin implies that such frankness must be severely limited to avoid such repercussions

In 1921, Lenin said:

> When we speak about our situation we speak the truth; we even exaggerate a bit to our disadvantage. In April, 1921, we said: Transport is falling, no food supplies are arriving. We wrote this openly in our newspapers, said it at thousands of meetings in the best halls of Moscow and Petrograd. The European spies immediately sent this by wire, and out there they were rubbing their hands and saying: "Go on, Poles, you see how bad things are there; we shall crush them right away." But we said the truth, sometimes exaggerating it to our disadvantage. . . . We must talk directly, without fearing the newspapers which are published in all the cities of the world. That is unimportant. We are not going to be silent about our difficult situation for that reason.[70]

9. Lenin implied that the degree of deception in the relations of the leadership with the Party and the masses must

be less than in those with the enemy. Stalin has abolished this difference.

* * *

Consistent with the rules concerning the need to be on guard against the enemy's efforts to deceive the Party (pars. 1 and 2), the Politburo shows a high degree of suspiciousness in its relations with other powers. It is particularly suspicious of expressions of friendliness toward it (pars. 3 and 4).

During World War II Stalin dissolved the Comintern, and the Soviet Union dissimulated its hostility toward the powers which were its allies from 1941 to 1945. The Politburo apparently felt that the gain from deceiving the West would be greater than any loss from reduced political consciousness in the communist world (pars. 7 and 8).

CHAPTER 13
VIOLENCE

1. Once it is clear that certain violent measures are necessary to the advance of communism, the amount of human misery involved becomes irrelevant.

In 1929, Stalin said:

> Now the expropriation of the kulaks is an integral part of the formation and development of the collective farms. That is why it is ridiculous and fatuous to expatiate today on the expropriation of the kulaks. We do not lament the loss of the hair of one who has been beheaded.[71]

2. The advance toward communism—and universal happiness—requires large human sacrifices.

In 1919, Lenin said:

> Dictatorship — that is a cruel, hard, bloody, painful word. . . .[72]

In 1921, he said:

> Until the final issue [between capitalism and communism] is decided the state of partial war will continue. We say: *"à la guerre comme à la guerre. . . ."*[73]

The high human cost of the transition to the new social order is an inevitable result of the high human cost of the present social order.

In 1918, Lenin said:

> . . . do they believe, in the camp of the bourgeoisie, that the revolution, which has been provoked by the war, by the unprecedented destruction, can proceed calmly, smoothly, in a pacific fashion, without torments, without the infliction of pain, without terror, without horror?[74]

And besides, there can be no great change without great cost.

In 1918, Lenin referred to the objections of "petty bourgeois" intellectuals to the suffering caused by the revolution, and said:

They had heard and admitted "in theory" that a revolution should be compared to an act of childbirth; but when it came to the point, they ... took flight. ... Take the descriptions of childbirth in literature, when the author's aim is to present a truthful picture of the severity, pain and horror of the act of travail. ... Human childbirth is an act which transforms the woman into an almost lifeless, bloodstained mass of flesh, tortured, tormented, and driven frantic by pain. But can the "type" that sees *only* this in love ... be regarded as a human being? Who would renounce love and procreation for *this* reason?[75]

And Stalin said to H. G. Wells in 1934:

The transformation of the world is a ... painful process.[76]

3. If the Party does not use violence against its enemies, it lays itself open to violence from its enemies.

In 1921, Lenin said:

Either the White Guard bourgeois terror of the American, British (Ireland), Italian (the fascists), German, Hungarian and other types, or Red proletarian terror. There is no middle course, no "third" course, nor can there be.[77]

In 1927, Stalin said:

And if it is necessary that somebody be "stained with blood," we shall exert all our efforts to make it some bourgeois country rather than the USSR.[78]

4. It is a lesser mistake to use too much violence than too little.

In 1918, Lenin said:

... Marx and Engels ... have seen as one of the causes of the collapse of the Paris Commune the fact that it did not utilize its armed power energetically enough to suppress the resistance of the exploiters.[79]

In 1927, Stalin said:

> ... we do not want to repeat the errors of the Paris communards. The communards of Paris were too lenient in dealing with Versailles. . . . They had to pay for their leniency, and when Thiers came to Paris, tens of thousands of workers were shot by the Versailles forces.[80]

* * *

These attitudes counteract the guilt which ruthlessness may evoke in Politburo members. Ruthlessness appears as grounded in the nature of politics itself, as a defense against ever-present attempts of the outer world to annihilate the Soviet Union, and is justified as a means to happiness under communism.

CHAPTER 14
THE DANGER OF ANNIHILATION

1. Although the enemy's insight into short-run developments may equal or surpass that of the Party, the Party excels in correctly predicting long-run developments.
2. Within these limits, Bolsheviks attribute to the main enemy (e.g., Wall Street) a degree of insight, skill, and energy equal to or surpassing that of the Party.
3. However, the phase of decline and fall (through which the enemy is held to be passing in this century) is believed to cause a certain amount of deterioration in these abilities.
4. All minor groups outside the Party's control are dominated by other major groups.

In 1925, Stalin said:

> ... the world is now divided into two camps: one of these camps is occupied by capitalism under Anglo-American leadership; the other is occupied by socialism under the leadership of the Soviet Union.[81]

In 1927, Stalin predicted that:

> ... two world centers will be formed: the socialist center, attracting to itself all the countries gravitating towards socialism, and the capitalist center attracting to itself all the countries gravitating towards capitalism. The fight between these two centers for the conquest of world economy will decide the fate of capitalism and communism throughout the whole world. . . .[82]

5. The most acute conflict between other states may at any moment be superseded by their combined attack on the Soviet Union.

In a February 18, 1918, session of the Central Committee, Lenin said:

It is possible that the Germans have reached an agreement with the French concerning not Poland but the overthrow of the Soviet government.[83]

In a letter written on October 3, 1918, he said:

The most kaleidoscopic changes are possible, there may be attempts to form an alliance of German and Anglo-French imperialism against the Soviet government.[84]

6. On the other hand, before the end of the Second World War, Bolshevik doctrine held that the unifying factors within the enemy camp tended to be neutralized by disruptive factors. It was also held that disruptive forces were stronger among the enemy than within the Soviet area.

In 1925, Stalin said:

In the capitalist camp, there is no unity of interests, no adequate centripetal force promoting consolidation. Within the capitalist camp, there is conflict of interests, a tendency towards disruption, a fight between victors and vanquished, a conflict among the victors, a dispute among all the imperialist countries for ... opportunities of making profits ... in the capitalist camp dissension and disintegration prevail ... in the socialist camp, consolidation is advancing, and there is an ever growing unification of interests against the common foe. . . .[85]

7. Because the existence of conflicts between strong enemies used to be regarded as a necessary condition for the preservation of power by the Party in its own area, the recent emergence of one dominant power outside of the Soviet Union is viewed as a grave danger.

In 1918, Lenin wrote about a similar situation:

... never has our situation been so dangerous. There are no longer two groups of imperialist marauders, mutually consuming and enfeebling each other and approximately of equal strength. There now remains only one group, the group of victors, the British and French imperialists, which is preparing to divide up the whole world among the capitalists; it has set itself the aim of overthrowing the Soviet regime in Russia at any cost. . . .[86]

8. In international relations it is one of the main tasks of the Party to know how to "utilize" conflicts between other states.

In 1920, Lenin said:

> ... we must know how to take advantage of the antagonism and contradictions existing among the imperialists. Had we not adhered to this rule, every one of us would have long ago been hanging from an aspen tree. . . .[87]

In 1921, Stalin referred to certain statements by Chicherin, then People's Commissar of Foreign Affairs:

> ... Comrade Chicherin is inclined to deny the existence of contradictions between the imperialist states, to exaggerate the international unanimity of the imperialists, and to overlook . . . contradictions which do . . . give rise to war. . . . Yet these contradictions do exist and it is on them that the activities of the People's Commissariat of Foreign Affairs are based. . . . The whole purpose of the existence of a People's Commissariat of Foreign Affairs is to take account of these contradictions, to use them as a basis, and to maneuver within these contradictions.[88]

9. Wherever possible, the Party must sharpen the conflict between other states.

In 1920, Lenin said:

> The practical part of Communist policy is . . . to incite one [enemy power] against the other. . . . we Communists must use one country against another.[89]

In a December 21, 1920, speech, Lenin developed the Soviet policy of offering economic concessions to American entrepreneurs in areas of the Soviet Far East then occupied by Japan. He explained that this policy was intended to bring about an intensification of the conflict between Japan and the United States. Although at the time of this speech no concessions had yet been granted, Lenin estimated that the consequences of this policy already were as follows:

... we [have] achieved a gigantic sharpening of the enmity between Japan and America and thereby an indubitable weakening of the offensive of Japan and America against us.[90]

10. Should an internecine conflict between other states exist —or have been brought about by the Party—the Party will intervene only at the end, and then decisively.

In 1925, Stalin said:

If a war were to begin, we would not sit still with idle hands. We will have to come out, but to come out after the others. And we shall come out for the purpose of throwing the decisive weight into the scales of fate. ...[91]

In 1939, Stalin interpreted British and French foreign policy in the same light:

[Their] policy of non-intervention reveals an eagerness ... to allow all the belligerents to sink deeply into the mire of war, to encourage them surreptitiously in this; to allow them to weaken and exhaust one another; and then, when they have become weak enough, to appear on the scene with fresh strength ... and to dictate conditions to the enfeebled belligerents.[92]

11. Any group not controlled by the Party, both at home and abroad, is an enemy.

In a letter written in 1902, Lenin instructs a Bolshevik in the technique of negotiating with a non-Bolshevik group of Russian Social Democrats:

... keep in mind that this is an unreliable friend (*and hence an enemy*).[93]

That is, there are no intermediate, neutral groups.

In 1933, Stalin said:

As for "neutral" collective farms, there is no such thing nor can there be. ... Under the conditions of the acute class struggle that is now going on in our Soviet land, there is no room for "neutral" collective farms. Under these circumstances, collective farms can be *either* Bolshevik *or* anti-Soviet. And if it is not we who are leading certain collective farms, that means that they are being led by anti-Soviet elements. There cannot be the slightest doubt about that.[94]

That is, the only good neighbor is the absolutely controlled neighbor.

In 1918, Lenin said that some "petty bourgeois" groups had declared their preference for a "neighborly" relation with the Soviet power. He commented:

Our task in relation to the petty-bourgeois democracy is . . . to test [it] in a way conforming with neighborly relations . . . under which the proletariat says: ". . . if you . . . intellectuals are really anxious to maintain neighborly relations with us, then be good enough to perform the tasks we assign you. If you do not, you will be . . . our enemies. . . . But if you maintain neighborly relations and perform these tasks . . . our support is secure. . . ." But now our whole purpose must be to treat the petty bourgeoisie as a good neighbor who is under the strict control of the [Soviet] state power.[95]

12. Most of the major policies of most of the governments abroad are intended to affect the Soviet Union.

In 1920, Lenin wrote:

. . . all events in world politics are . . . concentrated around one central point, viz., the struggle of the world bourgeoisie against the Soviet Russian Republic. . . .[96]

13. The enemy aims unceasingly at the annihilation of the Party, so that the survival (or victory) of the Party depends on an equal or superior counter-effort.

14. There is a tendency to believe that all of the ostensibly unconnected hostile actions of outside groups against the Party are governed by one master plan.

15. It is believed that these hostile acts are carried out in very devious ways. Thus, for instance, the enemy may request the Party to accede to an apparently trifling demand which, if granted, may turn out to be a major capitulation.

16. Small details in the policies of outside groups can give conclusive indications of an otherwise disguised hostile plan.

17. Until "socialist encirclement" of the rest of the world

is substituted for the "capitalist encirclement" of the Soviet Union, the Party will be weaker than its enemies and in constant danger of annihilation.

18. Between wars with the Soviet Union, the enemy calculates ways of intensifying hostile acts against the Soviet Union. In 1921, Lenin said:

> The international bourgeoisie, deprived of the possibility of waging open war against Soviet Russia, is waiting, always on the look out for the moment when conditions will permit the renewal of this war.[97]

In 1925, Stalin said:

> For the moment, the salient characteristic of the international situation is that the revolutionary movement has entered a period of calm, of truce. What is the meaning of this state of calm? It means ... above all that the attacks upon Soviet Russia have been reinforced. The imperialists have already begun preparing their onslaught against the Soviet Union. [98]

"We must be prepared for the fact that with the slightest change in the situation the imperialist pirates will again move against us." Hence, war is always imminent.

In 1933, Stalin said about the First Five Year Plan:

> We could not know just when the imperialists would attack the USSR ... ; but that they might attack us at any moment ... of that there could not be any doubt. That is why the Party was obliged to spur on the country, so as not to lose time, so as to make the utmost of the respite. . . . The Party could not afford to wait. . . .[99]

19. The enemy will actually make a number of all-out attempts to annihilate the Party.

In 1920, Lenin said:

> Hitherto the fate of all ... great revolutions has been decided by long series of wars. Our revolution is one of these great revolutions. We have passed through one period of war and we must prepare for a second.[100]

20. As the enemy passes through the phase of his decline and fall, the intensity of his attempts to annihilate the Party will increase.

In 1918, Lenin spoke about the "monstrous and savage frenzy in the face of death" on the part of "that wild beast, capitalism."

In 1933, Stalin said:

We must bear in mind that the growth of the power of the Soviet state will intensify the resistance of the last remnants of the dying classes. It is precisely because they are dying . . . that they will go on from one form of attack to other, sharper forms of attack. . . .[101]

Hence, as Lenin said in 1920:

While we were able to extricate ourselves from the first period of wars, we shall not extricate ourselves from the second period of wars so easily. . . .[102]

21. At the same time, the skillfulness of the enemy decreases.

In 1920, Lenin said:

Let the bourgeoisie rave, work itself into a frenzy, overdo things, commit acts of stupidity, take vengeance on the Bolsheviks in advance and endeavor to kill off . . . hundreds, thousands, and hundreds of thousands more of yesterday's and tomorrow's Bolsheviks. Acting thus, the bourgeoisie acts as all classes doomed by history have acted.[103]

* * *

Consistent with the attribution of a high degree of insight into short-run developments to its main enemies (par. 1), the Politburo regards "Wall Street" as blind to "the contradictions of capitalism" but as shrewd in limited political operations.

Consistent with the belief that all minor groups outside the Party are dominated by major groups (par. 4), the Politburo exaggerates the power of "Wall Street" domestically and internationally.

Consistent with pars. 7 and 10, the danger to the Soviet Union is held to increase as its power increases.

The foreign policy of the Politburo in 1939–1940 was consistent with pars. 8 through 10. It attempted to sharpen the tension between the Axis and the Western powers to increase the chances of an internecine conflict between them, during the course of which, particularly at the end, the Soviet Union would extend its domains.

The policy of the Politburo in Eastern Europe since 1944 has been consistent with par. 11. In this area, there has been a tendency to eliminate, or at least to restrict severely, any organization, however friendly, not controlled by the Party.

Consistent with par. 12, the Politburo tends to see anti-Soviet intents in policies of other powers, which are actually not concerned with the Soviet Union (e.g., in plans for postwar reorganization made during the last stages of the War and shortly afterward).

Consistent with the belief that the enemy is constantly aiming at the annihilation of the Party (pars. 13, 17, and 18), a real abatement of tension between the Communist and the non-Communist world is inconceivable to the Politburo.

CHAPTER 15
CONDUCT IN DEFEAT AND VICTORY

1. History indicates that recurrent setbacks are inevitable: "Wars which began and ended with an uninterrupted victorious advance have never occurred in world history, or else they have been very rare exceptions. This applies to ordinary wars. But what about wars . . . which decide the question of socialism or capitalism?"

In 1918, Lenin said:

To think that we shall not be thrown back is utopian.[104]

In 1925, Stalin said:

The epoch of the world revolution . . . may occupy years, or even decades. In the course of this period there will occur, nay, must occur, ebbs and flows in the revolutionary tide. . . . The first stage [of the revolution] lasted . . . from 1900 to 1917. . . . In 1905, there was a rise in the tide . . . from 1907 to 1912 the revolution was at low water mark, then, events in the Lena goldfields . . . mark a rise in the tide of the revolutionary movement which was, during the war, succeeded once more by an ebb. . . . February 1917 witnessed a fresh flow of the tide. . . . Each time the tide ebbed, the defeatists asserted that revolution was at an end. For all that, the revolution won through to victory in February 1917 [March, new calendar] in spite of the alternations of the tides. The second stage in our revolution dates from February 1917. . . . This stage . . . covered eight months . . . and . . . had its ebbs and flows . . . we had the surge of revolutionary feeling in the July demonstrations. The tide then ebbed. . . . Then came the Kornilov putsch. This was followed by a renewed rise in the revolutionary tide, which reached high water mark in the . . . October revolution. After the July setback, our defeatists chattered about the "liquidation" of the revolution. Nevertheless . . . the proletarian dictatorship was ... established. Since the October victory we have been living in the third stage of the revolution, during which our objective is the overthrow of the international bourgeoisie. ... We shall witness a succession of ebbs and flows in the revolutionary tide. For the time being the international revolutionary movement is in the declining phase; but ... this decline will yield ... to an upward surge which may end in the victory of the world proletariat. If, however, it should not end in victory, another decline will set in, to be followed in its turn by yet another revolutionary surge. Our defeatists maintain that the present ebb in the revolutionary tide marks the end of the revolution. They are mistaken now just as heretofore ... the revolution does not develop along a straight, continuous and upwardly aspiring line but along a zigzag path ... an ebb and flow in the tide....[105]

In 1927, Stalin said:

The fact that the Chinese revolution has not resulted in direct victory over imperialism, this fact cannot have decisive significance for the perspective of the revolution. Great popular revolutions never win through to the end on their first appearance. They grow and strengthen themselves by ebbs and flows. So it was everywhere, and in Russia too. So it will be in China.[106]

That is, major successes are often preceded by repeated failures: "We know that the transition from capitalism to socialism involves an extremely difficult struggle. But we are prepared ... to make a thousand attempts: having made a thousand attempts we shall go on to the next attempt." ". . . we shall act as we did in the Red Army: they may beat us a hundred times, but the hundred and first time we shall beat them all." "Not one of the problems that we have had to solve could be solved at one stroke; we had to make repeated attempts to solve them. Having suffered defeat, we tried again. . . ."

2. It is not possible to predict how strong an "ebb" will be, and how long it will last.

3. To achieve a major advance or final victory requires a length of time commensurate to the historical importance of

these events: ". . . the aim . . . [of the Party] is radically to transform the conditions of life of the whole of humanity, and . . . for that reason it is not permissible to be 'disturbed' by the question of the duration of the work."

4. A Bolshevik must always control any tendency to act inexpediently after a setback: ". . . a Marxist must be able to reckon with the most complicated and fantastic zigzag leaps of history. . . ." "Whatever the . . . vicissitudes of the struggle may be, however many partial zigzags it may be necessary to overcome (and there will be very many of them—we see from experience what tremendous twists the history of the revolution is making . . .), in order not to get lost in these zigzags and twists of history . . . in the periods of retreat, retirement or temporary defeat, or when history, or the enemy, throws us back . . . the . . . correct thing is not to cast out the old basic program."

5. Effective action depends on the belief that great danger threatens.

In 1920, Lenin said:

> When we fought and won on the war front, what was one of the most powerful impulses that served to magnify our strength and our energy tenfold? It was the realization of danger. Everybody asked: Can the landlords and capitalists return to Russia? And the reply was that they could. We therefore multiplied our efforts a hundredfold and we were victorious.[107]

A Bolshevik must always control the strong tendency to become "complacent" after a success. ". . . [with us] a few successes are sufficient for people to forget about defects, to calm down and to put on airs. Two or three big successes—and already the ocean is at one's knees. Two or three more big successes, and airs are put on: 'We will bury them under our hats!' " [A Russian slogan in the war against Japan, 1904–1905.]

6. Complacency will cause the Party to abandon the principle of pursuit (i.e., to overlook possible further advantages)

and thus cause later losses.

In 1924, Stalin said about Lenin:

> At the . . . London 1907 Party Congress the Bolsheviks were victors [after having been the minority in the Stockholm Congress in 1906]. Then I saw Lenin for the first time in the role of victor. Usually victory makes . . . leaders dizzy. . . . Most often they begin . . . to celebrate the victory, to rest on their laurels. Lenin . . . on the contrary, became particularly vigilant and cautious after victory. I remember how Lenin at that time stubbornly explained to the delegates: "The first matter at hand is not to be carried away by victory . . . ; the second matter is to consolidate this victory; the third to defeat the enemy completely as he has only been beaten but is not destroyed." Lenin . . . laughed at those delegates who light-heartedly affirmed that "the Mensheviks are finished." It was not difficult for him to show that the Mensheviks still possessed certain strong points in the workers' movement, that one should fight with them skilfully, and in all circumstances avoid an overestimation of one's own forces, and particularly an underestimation of those of the enemy.[108]

7. Or, "complacency" will cause the Party, "dizzy with success," to attempt excessive advances with inadequate preparation: ". . . successes also have their seamy side; especially when they are achieved with comparative 'ease,' 'unexpectedly,' so to speak. Such successes sometimes induce a spirit of conceit and arrogance: 'We can do anything!' 'We can win hands down!' People are often intoxicated by such successes, they become dizzy with success . . . they reveal a tendency to overestimate their own strength and to underestimate the strength of the enemy. . . . In such cases no care is taken to *consolidate* the successes achieved and to *utilize* them systematically for the purpose of advancing further."

In 1923, Stalin wrote:

> . . . in 1920, at the time of the war with the Poles . . . we underestimated the force of the national factor in Poland and became carried away by the easy success of our impressive advance. We undertook a task which was beyond our

forces, to break through into Europe through Warsaw; we induced the union against the Soviet army of the enormous majority of the Polish population. Thus, we created a situation which undid the successes of the Soviet army . . . and undermined the prestige of the Soviet power in the west.[109]

* * *

Consistent with the acceptance of the inevitability of recurrent setbacks and the slow working of historical processes (pars. 1 and 3), the Politburo does not necessarily expect to achieve quick successes. In its attempts to advance, such as those directed against Berlin for some years, it is prepared to be repulsed at any given moment.

Consistent with the rules concerning the dangers of complacency (pars. 6 and 7), when the Politburo is in a position of advantage (as it was during the latter phases of the Second World War) it constantly tests the feasibility of further advance.

CHAPTER 16
ADVANCE

1. The only way in which the Party can achieve gains is by intense "struggle."

2. The Party must take possession of every no man's land; otherwise the enemy will.

3. However "backward" a country may be, the Party must always strive to gain control over it.

4. In periods of crisis the Party is likely to advance abruptly from a position of weakness to one of strength.

In an open letter to Boris Souvarine, written in December, 1916, Lenin said:

> The really revolutionary internationalists are numerically weak? You don't say so! Let us take as example France in 1780 and Russia in 1900. In both cases, conscious and decided revolutionaries—in the first case, representatives of the bourgeoisie . . . in the second case, representatives of the . . . proletariat—were extremely weak numerically. They were lone wolves, at the most, one out of ten thousand, or even one out of a hundred thousand in their class. But after a few years, these same lone wolves, that same allegedly so insignificant minority led the masses, millions and tens of millions of people. . . . When in November 1914 our Party announced the necessity of a split with the opportunists . . . this announcement appeared to many merely as sectarian madness of people who had definitely broken with life and reality. Two years passed and look what is happening.[110]

5. There are rare occasions which offer unusual possibilities for making great advances. The Party must learn to seize them.

6. On the other hand, no advance, however small, should be neglected.

7. The Party must concentrate on actually carrying out a

small advance rather than permit itself to become absorbed in fantasies of grandiose advances that are unfeasible at the moment.

In a letter written in 1921, Lenin commented on a paper by V. P. Milyutin proposing the immediate introduction of a single over-all economic plan:

> Milyutin writes rubbish about the Plan. . . . We are poor, starving, ruined beggars. A complete . . . plan for us now would be a bureaucratic utopia. Do not run after it! The most important parts of it should be taken bit by bit, and the minimum number of enterprises should be organized at once, without delaying a day, or even an hour.[111]

8. Intermissions between advances are necessary.

In 1930, Stalin said about agricultural policy:

> Those who are babbling about a retreat . . . do not know the laws of an offensive. They do not understand that an offensive *without* the positions already captured *having been consolidated* is an offensive that is doomed to failure. When can an offensive be successful in the military sphere, let us say? When the people concerned do not confine themselves to a headlong advance along the whole line, but try at the same time to *consolidate* the positions captured, to *regroup* their forces in accordance with the changed circumstances, *to bring up* the rear and *to move up* reserves.[112]

9. The Party must not allow enemy "provocation" to induce an untimely attempt to advance.

In 1927, Stalin affirmed that the British government was preparing war against the Soviet Union and said:

> The first overt blow was dealt by the . . . British government in Peking when it attacked the Soviet consulate. . . . This was supposed . . . to drag the USSR into a war with China. This blow miscarried. . . . The third overt blow was dealt in Warsaw by the organization of the assassination of [the Soviet ambassador] Voikov. [This] assassination . . . was supposed to . . . drag the USSR into a warlike conflict with Poland. This blow, too, miscarried. . . . The task consists in continuing the peaceful policy of the Soviet govern-

ment . . . regardless of the provocative sallies of our enemies, regardless of the pinpricks against our prestige. Provocateurs from the enemy camp provoke, and will continue to provoke, us, affirming that our peaceful policy is caused by our weakness. . . . This sometimes makes some among those of our comrades who are disposed to let themselves be provoked explode, and they demand the application of "decided" measures. This is a weakness of the nerves. This is a lack of endurance. We cannot and we shall not dance to the piping of our enemies. We must go our own way. . . .[113]

10. The Party must never show "adventurism" in its attempts to advance; that is, it must never risk already conquered major positions for the sake of uncertain further gains.

On January 20, 1918, Lenin said:

. . . it would be a quite impermissible tactic to risk the already begun socialist revolution in Russia simply because of the hope that the German revolution will break out in a very short time, in a few weeks. Such a tactic would be adventurist. We have no right to assume such a risk.[114]

On January 24, 1918, Lenin discussed the proposal that war against Germany should be resumed in order to maximize the chances of the German revolution:

But Germany is still only pregnant with revolution, while with us a perfectly healthy child has already seen the light of the world, a child which we may kill by beginning the war.[115]

11. Within the plan of advance, there must always be provision for retreat: ". . . we must prepare for ourselves the possibility of retreat . . . all the parties which are preparing to pass to the direct onslaught upon capitalism in the near future, must now also think of ensuring the possibility of retreat for themselves."

12. The Party must cease its attempts to advance if, and only if, previous experiences have unmistakably shown that it would be wasteful or dangerous to continue. That is, the Party must not run its head against a wall; on the other hand, the

Party must have attempted with full force to break it down before it can cease its offensive. "Marxism is not against compromises in general, it regards their utilization as necessary. But this does not exclude the fact that Marxism . . . struggles against compromises by the exertion of all its energy. Not to understand this apparent contradiction means to ignore the elements of Marxism."

13. The Party must avoid the danger not only of exaggerating but also of underestimating the difficulties of overcoming obstacles in its path. The first attitude is that of "bowing to what exists at the present time"; the second is that of "breaking with reality." "It is indispensable that the Party know how to combine in its work an irreconcilable revolutionary spirit (which should not be confused with revolutionary adventurism!) with maximum elasticity and capacity to maneuver (which should not be confused with a tendency towards passive adaptation)!"

14. If the Party is forced to abandon an attempt to advance, it must use the experience gained in this attempt to create new conditions for another and successful advance. Like the enemy, the Party never "disarms."

15. The Party must be prepared to change from a forward movement of "assault" ("frontal attack") to a "siege" or a "detour" as soon as it is evident that the assault has failed.

In 1921, Lenin, discussing the transition from war communism to the New Economic Policy, said:

> . . . I should like to take for . . . comparison an episode in the Russo-Japanese war . . . the capture of Port Arthur by . . . General Nogi. The main thing that interests me in this episode is that the capture of Port Arthur was accomplished in two . . . different stages. The first stage was that of furious assault, which ended in failure and cost the celebrated Japanese commander very heavy losses. The second stage was the . . . slow method of siege . . . and after a time it was precisely by this method that the problem of capturing the fortress was solved . . . the storming of Port Arthur . . . was the only possible tactics to adopt in the conditions

... prevailing ... in the beginning of operations ... for without testing the strength of the fortress by the practical attempt to carry it by assault, without testing the power of resistance of the enemy, there would have been no grounds for adopting the ... prolonged ... method of struggle, which, by the very fact that it was prolonged, harboured a number of other dangers.[116]

In the same speech, Lenin recalled the reaction of the Russian "bourgeoisie" to the moderate policy of the Party immediately after the seizure of power:

... the bourgeois class resorted to every device to provoke us into the most extreme manifestation of desperate struggle. Was it strategically correct from the enemy's point of view? Of course it was correct. Because how could the bourgeoisie be expected to submit to an absolutely new ... proletarian power without first testing its strength by means of a direct assault? ... From the point of view of protecting its interests, the bourgeoisie acted quite rightly. If it had even a crumb of hope of settling the fundamental question by the most effective means—war—it could not agree ... to the partial concessions the Soviet government gave it with a view to making a more gradual transition to the new system.[117]

16. One function of an advance is to provide leeway in case of subsequent retreats. Thus any advance has a defensive as well as an offensive rationale.

In 1922, Lenin said:

... we are retreating because we have won enough to enable us to hold the necessary positions. We have won enormous positions, and had we not won these positions in the period of 1917–1921, we should not have had any room to retreat geographically, economically and politically.[118]

In 1924, Stalin said about periods of retreat:

The proletarian power is able to adopt such a policy because, and only because, the sweep of the revolution in the preceding period ... allowed sufficient leeway to permit of retreat.

... The revolutionary conquests of the proletariat ... serve
as accumulated reserves in the hands of the proletariat.[119]

* * *

Consistent with the belief that "intense struggle" is essential
for any advances (par. 1), it is inconceivable to the Politburo
that its aims could be advanced in an atmosphere relatively free
of international tension.

Politburo policy in the areas between its domains and the
rest of the world since 1944 has been consistent with the rule
calling for the occupation of every no man's land (par. 2).

Politburo policy in Asia since 1945 has been consistent with
the belief that the Party should strive to control even the most
backward countries (par. 3).

The development of the Chinese Communist Party would
appear to the Politburo as consistent with the rule that rapid
advances from weakness to strength can occur in periods of
crisis (par. 4).

Presumably the Politburo regarded the destruction of the
Wehrmacht in 1945 as one of the rare occasions when unusual
possibilities for great advances are offered (par. 5). Another
such occasion might be created if the Politburo developed
thermonuclear weapons ahead of the United States.

Politburo policy outside of Eastern Asia, from 1948 to the
present time, has been consistent with (pars. 6 and 7) (e.g.,
the persistent fight for small economic advantages in Austria
and Iran).

Consistent with (par. 8), the Politburo presumably regards
the situation prevailing in Western Europe since 1948 as an
intermission between a past and a future advance.

Consistent with the rule against "adventurism" (par. 10),
the Soviet Army has not attempted any further expansion in
Europe since 1945.

Politburo behavior in Berlin, Northern Greece, and Northern
Iran since the end of the war was consistent with the rule
against continuing dangerous or wasteful advances (par. 12).

Politburo policies toward Western Europe from 1948 to the present time (as against those of 1945–1948) have been consistent with par. 15. When it became clear that the United States would forestall (or react with war to) a seizure of power by any Communist Party in Western Europe or an advance of the Soviet Army beyond its 1945 positions, the immediate objectives of the Politburo in Western Europe became more limited.

CHAPTER 17
EXERTION OF PRESSURE

1. Only by putting the greatest pressure on an outside group can the Party induce it to modify its policies in ways that are most useful to the Party.

In a letter in 1903, Lenin outlined the policy that his fraction within the Russian Social Democratic Labor Party should adopt toward an opposing fraction (the Bund) at an impending Congress:

... we ask you strongly to prepare everywhere, and among all persons concerned, the basis for the struggle with the Bund. ... Without stubborn struggle, the Bund will not give up its position. Only a firm resolve on our side to go to the end, to the point of expelling the Bund from the Party, will, no doubt, compel it to give in.[120]

In another letter in 1903, Lenin wrote about the same issue:

We must impress over and over again on everybody that we must prepare war on the Bund if we want to have peace with it. War at the Congress, war up to a split—at any cost. Only then will the Bund doubtlessly give in.[121]

In 1928, Stalin said:

Some think that agreement with the middle peasants can be brought about by abandoning the fight against the kulak, or by slackening this fight; because, they say, the fight against the kulak may frighten away a section of the middle peasantry, its well-to-do section. Others think that agreement with the middle peasants can be brought about by abandoning the work of organizing the poor peasants, or by slackening this work; because, they say, the organization of the poor peasants means singling out the poor peasants, and this may frighten the middle peasants away from us. ...

Such people forget the Marxian thesis that the middle peasants are a vacillating class, that agreements with the middle peasants can be durable only if a determined fight is carried on against the kulaks and if the work among the poor peasants is intensified; that unless these conditions are adhered to, the middle peasants may swing to the side of the kulaks....[122]

2. One type of useful pressure is intense and incessant expression (or, if necessary, simulation) of hostility.

In 1904, Lenin described what should be the conduct of the Social Democratic Party toward the "bourgeois" opponents of tsarism:

How else can we imbue liberal democracy with courage than by ruthless controversy and ... destructive criticism of its half-heartedness in questions of democracy?[123]

In 1908, Lenin wrote, when advocating a coalition between the proletariat (i.e., the Party) and the revolutionary peasantry as represented by such a party as the Trudoviks:

A "coalition" of the proletariat and the peasantry for the purpose of obtaining a victory over their common enemy can be realized not by throwing amorous glances towards the Trudoviks, but only by ruthless criticism of their weaknesses and vacillations....[124]

3. Threats are useful in the same way.

In 1905, Lenin advised some Bolsheviks who were to appear in court:

On the question of lawyers: one must crack the whip against the lawyers and put them under a state of siege, for this intellectual gentry often does dirty things. One must say in advance: If you bastard commit even the smallest indecency or *political opportunism* (e.g., if you were to talk of the immaturity or incorrectness of socialism, of enthusiasm, of the *refusal of violence by the social democrats,* of the peaceful character of their teaching and their movement, etc., or of anything similar), then I, the accused, will immediately

publicly interrupt you, will call you a skunk, will declare
that I renounce such defence, etc. Such threats must be
acted upon.[125]

4. In attempting to obtain concessions, anything less than
the exertion of maximum pressure is ineffective and will bring
humiliation to the Party.

In 1907, Lenin reviewed the relations between the
tsarist government and the Russian liberals since the
outbreak of the revolution:

The liberal leaders of the first and second Duma demon-
strated to the people excellently the type of "struggle" in
which one behaves legally and goes down on one's knees.
This resulted in the absolutist feudal lords abolishing the
constitutional paradise of the liberal chatterboxes with one
stroke of the pen and laughing derisively at the subtle diplomacy of these politicians, who cooled their heels in the
waiting rooms of the ministers.[126]

5. A group subjected to maximum pressure by the Party is
not expected to react with intensified hostility; if it does, however, it is not expected to change its policy in a way unfavorable
to the Party.

In 1902, Lenin refused to tone down his controversy
with other anti-tsarist groups and affirmed that verbal
violence would not reduce the probability of an alliance between the Social Democrats and those groups:

It is time to understand the simple truth that a ... common
battle against the common enemy is not insured by cheap
political tricks ... by the conventional lie of mutual diplo-
matic recognition—but rather by the actual participation in
battle. ... Only people who confuse politics with cheap
political tricks can believe that the "tone" of a polemic is
capable of preventing a real political alliance.[127]

If the Party's heavy pressure evokes rage, it is an indication
that the Party's policy is correct; a friendly reaction should be
taken to indicate an incorrect policy (e.g., a weak one).

In 1905, Lenin said:

... the liberal bourgeois recognize the proletariat as heroic *just because* this proletariat, which has dealt tsarism a blow, is not yet strong enough, not yet social democratic enough, *to obtain in battle* the freedom it [the proletariat] wants ... we have no reasons to be proud of the current liberal flattery.[128]

In 1927, Stalin said:

The slander which has been circulated about the GPU knows no bounds. And what does that mean? It means that the GPU is properly defending ... the Revolution. The sworn enemies of the Revolution curse the GPU. Hence, it follows that the GPU is doing the right thing.[129]

In 1931, he said:

See how ... Fish in America, Churchill in England, Poincaré in France, fume and rave against our Party! Why do they fume and rave in this way? Because the policy of our party is correct, because it is achieving success after success.[130]

6. The Party must keep on guard against apparently friendly outside groups. Friendliness may serve as a screen behind which the enemy works "to lay a trap," "to worm itself into the Party's confidence," or to disunite the Party. "Conciliation is impossible in politics, and only out of . . . simplicity . . . can the time-honored . . . methods of . . . yielding the unimportant in order to preserve the essential, giving with one hand and taking back with the other, be taken for conciliation."

*   *   *

Politburo behavior toward the Western Powers from 1944 to the present time has been consistent with pars. 1 through 6.

As a result of the belief that a group subjected to maximum pressure by the Party will not react with increased hostility (par. 5), the Politburo has probably underestimated the effect of its hostile attitudes on American rearmament and on the extent of American commitments abroad.

CHAPTER 18
RESISTANCE TO ATTACK

1. The Party leadership must not be indignant about enemy attacks, but must always expect the worst, as corresponding to the enemy's interests.

In March, 1939, Stalin said, discussing British and French foreign policy:

> Far be it from me to moralize on the policy of non-intervention, to talk of treason, treachery, and so on. . . . Politics is politics, as the . . . bourgeois diplomats say.[131]

2. It is impossible by a moral or rational appeal to persuade an enemy to reduce his enmity.

In 1929, Stalin said:

> . . . Bukharin's group hope to persuade the class enemy voluntarily to forego its interest and voluntarily to deliver its grain surpluses. They hope that the kulak . . . who is able to hold out by selling other products and who conceals his grain surpluses—they hope that this kulak will give us his grain surpluses voluntarily at our purchase prices. Have they lost their senses? . . . Do they know with what derision the kulaks treat our people and the Soviet government at village meetings called to assist the grain purchases? Have they heard a fact like the one, for instance, that happened in Kazakstan, when one of our agitators tried for two hours to pursuade the holders of grain to deliver that grain for feeding the country, and a kulak stepped forward with pipe in mouth and said: "Do us a little dance, young fellow, and I will let you have a couple of puds of grain." . . . Try to persuade people like that. Class is class, comrades. You cannot get away from that truth.[132]

3. The Party is always warding off attempts to annihilate it, and at the same time it is working for victory. In order to preserve its existence and to achieve its goal, the Party must always

77

exert maximum energy. ". . . we must not lull the Party, but sharpen its vigilance; we must not lull it to sleep, but keep it ready for action; not disarm it, but arm it; not demobilize it, but hold it in a state of mobilization. . . ."

4. Enemy attacks must be perceived and resisted in their earliest beginnings.

5. Such beginnings might lie, for example, in ostensibly minor slights to Party prestige. Although the Party must not consider prestige to be valuable in itself, such apparently minor incidents must be reacted to strongly, unless the relation of forces is unfavorable.

6. ". . . it is our habit to reply to attacks, not by defence, but by counterattacks."

> In a 1904 letter to the Bolshevik-dominated Central Committee in Russia, Lenin wrote:
>
> . . . the Martovite [Menshevik] pressure must be repulsed by similar pressure (and not by a disgusting mouthing about peace, etc.). . . . I really think we have bureaucrats and formalists, and not revolutionaries, serving on the Central Committee. The Martovites are spitting in their faces, but they merely wipe their faces and moralize to me that it is useless trying to fight![133]

7. The coexistence of the Party and of its enemies is an unstable situation; at any moment the question as to who will annihilate whom may come up for decision.

> In 1938, Stalin wrote about developments after the "July days" of 1917:
>
> The dual power had come to an end. The Soviets . . . had refused to take over full power and had therefore lost all power.[134]

If the Party's power is below a certain critical level of strength, the Party is in danger of being annihilated by the enemy. If its power is above this level, the Party can move toward annihilating the enemy.

> In 1931, Stalin said:
>
> . . . Lenin said during the October Revolution: "Either perish

or overtake and outstrip the advanced capitalist countries."
... either we do it, or they crush us.[135]

The Party must reverse the Russian history of always being beaten.

In 1931, Stalin said:

To slacken the tempo [of economic growth in the Soviet Union] would mean to fall behind. And those who fall behind get beaten. But we do not want to be beaten. No, we refuse to be beaten! One feature of the history of old Russia was the continual beatings she suffered for falling behind, for her backwardness. She was beaten by the Mongol khans. She was beaten by the Turkish beys. She was beaten by the Polish and Lithuanian gentry. She was beaten by the British and French capitalists. She was beaten by the Japanese barons. All beat her—for her backwardness; for military backwardness, for cultural backwardness, for political backwardness, for industrial backwardness, for agricultural backwardness. She was beaten because to do so was practicable and could be done with impunity. Do you remember the words of the prerevolutionary poet: "You are poor and abundant, mighty and impotent, Mother Russia!" These words of the old poet were well learned by those gentlemen. They beat her, saying, "You are abundant," for one can enrich oneself at your expense. They beat her, saying, "You are poor and impotent," so you can be beaten and plundered with impunity. Such is the law of the exploiters —to beat the backward and the weak. It is the jungle law of capitalism. You are backward, you are weak—therefore you are wrong; hence, you can be beaten and enslaved. You are mighty—therefore you are right; hence, we must be wary of you. That is why we must no longer lag behind.[136]

8. The only safe enemy is one whose power has been completely destroyed. If the enemy is left with any power at all, he may recover and reverse the situation in a future battle. But, while it is imperative to annihilate the last remnants of a defeated enemy, it is also difficult to do so.

Hence the Party must rigorously apply the principle of pursuit toward its enemies. "If your adversary is numbed by the first attack, don't let fatigue prevent you from hitting him again, double the force and the number of your blows."

In 1919, Lenin said:

> The French Revolution has been called great precisely because ... it was a businesslike revolution which, having overthrown the monarchists, annihilated them.[137]

The Party must combat the Russian tendency to over-optimism and inaction after merely partial victory over a still dangerous enemy who should be quickly destroyed.

On June 12, 1920, Lenin said:

> Despite the successes which we have had on the Polish front ... we must exert all our forces. In war ... the most dangerous thing is to underestimate the enemy.... This ... can lead to defeat. That is the worst trait of Russians: it expresses itself in instability and slovenliness. It is important not only to begin but also to persevere and to maintain one's position and our Russian does not understand that. Only training of many years ... will cure the Russian working masses of this bad habit. We have beaten Kolchak, Denikin and Yudenich, but we have not known how to destroy them completely. Wrangel in the Crimea remains. We said to ourselves: now we are certainly stronger—and hence a whole set of slovenly acts were committed. In the meantime, Britain gives aid to Wrangel ... a few days ago Wrangel landed troops and occupied Melitopol. True enough, according to the latest news we have reconquered the city, but we had abandoned it in a very ignominious fashion just because we were strong. Because Yudenich, Kolchak and Denikin have been beaten, the Russian begins to reveal his nature. He ceases to exert himself and the cause is lost.... These are fundamental traits of the Russian character. Nothing has yet been finished but he already begins ... to let himself go.... I don't know what the Russian will have to do to liberate himself from these mistakes and stupidities. We already once thought the war was finished, despite the fact that we had not completely destroyed the enemy, and had left Wrangel in the Crimea.[138]

*   *   *

Consistent with par. 3, the motivation of Politburo moves, from 1945 to the present time, has not only been offensive, but also defensive.

Soviet concern with the procedural aspects of international conferences has been consistent with the belief that enemy attacks should be resisted from the first (par. 4), and Soviet "touchiness" has been consistent with the belief that even minor slights to Party prestige should be reacted to strongly (par. 5).

The Politburo habit of raising countercharges to charges levelled against it (e.g., in the U.N.) is consistent with the practice of resorting to counterattack rather than to defensive tactics (par. 6).

Politburo policy in Eastern Europe from 1944 to the present time has been consistent with par. 8. It has shown a determination to destroy, as far as practicable, any potentially hostile organizations.

CHAPTER 19

RETREAT

1. Mastery in the skill of retreating is as necessary as mastery in the skill of advancing.

In 1922, Lenin said:

> When it was necessary—according to the objective situation in Russia as well as the whole world—to advance, to attack the enemy with supreme boldness, rapidity, decisiveness, we did so attack. When it will be necessary, we will know how to do this again and again. . . . And when, in the spring of 1921, it appeared that the advance guard of the revolution was threatened by the danger of becoming isolated from the mass of the people . . . then we resolved unanimously and firmly to retreat. And for the past year we have in general retreated in revolutionary order. Proletarian revolutions . . . will not be able to fulfil their tasks without combining the skill in . . . attack with the skill in retreating in revolutionary order.[139]

2. ". . . there are retreats and retreats. There are times when a party or an army has to retreat because it has suffered defeat. . . . But there are other times, when in its advance a victorious party or army runs too far ahead, without providing itself with an adequate base in the rear. . . . So as not to lose connection with its base, an experienced party or army generally finds it necessary in such cases to fall back a little, to draw closer to and establish better contact with its base. . . ."

3. The Party must not avoid the unfavorable aspects of reality. It must face the full gravity of adverse circumstances which make a retreat necessary and involve heavy losses.

In 1918, Lenin said about the Brest-Litovsk peace:

> We were forced to sign a "Tilsit peace." We must not deceive ourselves. We must have the courage to look the

unadorned bitter truth straight in the face. We must measure to the bottom that abyss of defeat, of dismemberment, of enslavement, of humiliation into which we have been pushed.[140]

4. Feelings of distress about retreating must not keep the Party from executing an expedient retreat.

In 1921 (in connection with the New Economic Policy, which was regarded as a retreat), Lenin said:

This [commerce] is a discovery which is highly disagreeable for Communists. It may well be that this discovery is extraordinarily disagreeable, it is even indubitable that it is disagreeable. But if we want to govern our actions by considerations of agreeableness or disagreeableness, we shall have fallen to the level of those "almost" socialists, which we ourselves have sufficiently seen in ... the provisional government of Kerensky. ... Our strength will always be a capacity to take account of the real relationships and not to fear them, however disagreeable they may be.[141]

In 1922, Lenin said about this same "retreat":

A retreat is a difficult matter, especially for revolutionaries who are accustomed to advance, especially when they have been accustomed to advance with enormous success for several years, especially if they are surrounded by revolutionaries in other countries yearning for the time when they can start the offensive. Seeing that we were retreating, several of them in a disgraceful and childish manner shed tears, as was the case of the last Enlarged Plenum of the Executive Committee of the Communist International. ... several of the comrades burst into tears because, just imagine, the good Russian Communists were retreating. Perhaps it is now difficult for me to understand west European psychology, although I spent quite enough years in those beautiful democratic countries as a political exile. Perhaps it is so difficult for them to understand this that they shed tears over it. We, at any rate, have no time for sentiment.[142]

In a retreat (and at all other times) depression and agitation must be avoided or controlled.

In 1921, again referring to the New Economic Policy, Lenin said:

> One must not surrender to depression, one must not set aside the real question by agitational exclamations....[143]

Similarly, conceptions of dignity must not keep the Party from executing an expedient retreat.

In 1918, Lenin said, advocating the acceptance of the German peace terms:

> ... if you are not inclined to crawl in the mud on your belly, you are not a revolutionary, but a chatterbox....[144]

Also, he said:

> One should not be guided by the feeling of a participant in a duel who draws his sword and exclaims: I must die because I am compelled to sign a humiliating peace.[145]

5. The Party must retreat if, and only if, the experience gained in attempting to hold an attacked position shows that not to retreat would involve greater losses. That is, "in the case of clearly disadvantageous conditions it is the duty of the serious revolutionary to avoid battle."

6. By such a retreat the Party gains time, which works in its favor.

In 1923, Stalin said:

> ... there are moments when one must neglect tactical successes, consciously assume tactical minuses and losses for the sake of securing future strategic pluses. This is often the case in war, when one side wants to save the cadres of its army and lead them out from under the blows of the excellent forces of the enemy. Then it begins a planned retreat and gives up, without fighting, whole cities and areas for the sake of winning time and collecting forces for new decisive battles in the future. This was the situation in Russia in 1918 at the time of the German offensive when our Party was forced to accept the Brest peace which was an enormous minus from the point of view of the immediate political effect at that moment. The Party did this for the sake of preserving the alliance with the peasants thirsting

for peace, in order to gain a breathing space, to create a new army, and thus to secure future strategic pluses.[146]

In unfavorable situations a small gain in time is better than none.

In a March 8, 1918, speech at the Seventh Party Congress, Lenin said to the "Left Communists" who had delayed the conclusion of peace with Germany:

Had you pursued a correct strategy we would have had a month's respite, but as you pursued a wrong strategy, we had only five days respite—and even that is good.[147]

7. Any degree of retreat is preferable to risking the annihilation of the Party or the total loss of state power. In a March 1, 1918, *Pravda* article, Lenin discussed the affirmation, in a resolution by the "left" Moscow District Bureau of the Party, that in case of the acceptance of the German peace conditions the Soviet power would become "something purely formal":

... the Soviet power is not going to become something purely formal. It is not going to become that when the conqueror is in Pskov and imposes on us a ten billion tribute in grain, in ore and money, but also if the enemy will be in Nizhni Novgorod and in Rostov-on-Don and will impose a tribute of twenty billions on us.[148]

In a March 7, 1918, speech at the Seventh Party Congress, Lenin said:

... without a German revolution we are doomed—perhaps not in Petrograd, not in Moscow, but in Vladivostok, in more remote places to which perhaps we shall have to retreat. . . .[149]

In a March 14, 1918, speech, Lenin said:

This period is a period of heavy defeat, of retreat, a period during which we must save at least a small part of our positions by retreating. . . .[150]

In 1921, Lenin said about the relationship of the Soviet regime to the peasantry:

... we shall make every possible concession within the
limits of retaining power. . . .[151]

As long as the Party and its state power (even in a reduced
area and to a reduced degree) are preserved, not everything is
lost. From the remote bases to which it may have retreated to
preserve its existence, the Party will in time launch a successful
counteroffensive. But: "In order to build socialism one must
. . . exist."

There is always a way out.

On March 12, 1918, Lenin said about the situation
created by the German peace conditions:

> It is not true that we have no way out and that we have to
> choose between a going down "without glory" by the hard
> peace, and a going down "in glory" in a hopeless battle.[152]

8. In a retreat every point must be contested as long and as
intensely as possible, and the withdrawal of forces must occur
only when the advancing enemy is about to become overwhelm-
ing. Such last-minute retreats are apt to be sudden and quick.

On February 21, 1918, Lenin said about the proper
conduct of the Soviet government toward Germany:

> ... one had to determine the "appropriate" moment for
> maneuvering and agitating—as long as this was possible—as
> well as for the cessation of all maneuvers at the moment
> when the question was put with full sharpness.[153]

9. An otherwise necessary retreat may create a vicious circle,
as it may put the enemy in a more favorable position to press
for yet another retreat, and the Party in an even worse position
to resist. But if the Party is alive to this danger, it will usually
be able to obviate it.

In 1921, Lenin said:

> ... I will touch upon the question which is engaging every-
> body's mind. If today, in the autumn and winter of 1921,
> we are making *another* retreat, when will the retreat stop?
> ... When we were concluding the Brest peace we were
> asked: "If you yield this, that and the other to German

imperialism, when will the concessions stop, and what guar-
antee is there that they will stop? And in making these
concessions, are you not making our position more dangerous?" Of course, we are making our position more dangerous. . . . There is not a moment in time of war when we are
not surrounded by danger. And what is the dictatorship of
the proletariat? It is war, much more cruel, much more prolonged . . . than any war has ever been. Here danger threatens at every step.[154]

*   *   *

The over-all situation since 1943 has been so favorable to
the Politburo as to render inoperative most of the rules indicated in this chapter. However, limited retreats by the Politburo
in Northern Iran, Northern Greece, and Berlin seem to have
been consistent with the beliefs indicated here.

CHAPTER 20
DEALS

1. Any agreements between the Party and outside groups must be regarded as aiding the future liquidation of these groups and as barriers against the liquidation of the Party by them. Thus, " 'Reformism,' 'the policy of agreement' and 'particular agreements' are different matters . . . with the Mensheviks agreements are transformed into a system, into a policy of agreement, while with the Bolsheviks only particular concrete agreements are acceptable, and are not made into a policy of agreement."

Therefore there is no essential difference between coming to an ostensibly amicable arrangement with an outside group or using violence against it; they are both tactics in an over-all strategy of attack.

In 1920, Lenin said, with reference to Soviet plans for granting economic "concessions" to foreign entrepreneurs:

> The major theme of my speech will be the proof of two points, namely, first, that every war is the continuation of the policy conducted in peace, only by other means; second, that the concessions which we grant, which we are forced to grant, are the continuation of war in another form, by other means. . . . It would be a great mistake to believe that a peaceful agreement about concessions is—a peaceful agreement with capitalists. This agreement is equivalent to war. . . .[155]

2. When an attempt by the enemy, or by the Party, to advance by violent means has failed, the conditions for an effective agreement between the Party and the enemy come into existence.

88

In 1920, Lenin said:

... every attempt to start war on us will mean for the states resorting to war that the terms they will get after and as a result of the war will be worse than those that they could have got without war or before war. This has been proved in the case of several states. ... And thanks to this our relations with neighboring states are steadily improving. ... Peace on such a basis has every chance of being ... durable. ...[156]

In 1921, Lenin said:

Can we obtain goods now? We can, because our international economic position has improved enormously. We are fighting against international capital, which, on seeing our republic, said: "These are robbers, reptiles" (these are literally the very words that were conveyed to me by an English sculptress who heard them uttered by one of the most influential politicians). ... We said: If you are a mighty world power, if you are world capital, if you say "reptile," and have all the powers of technique at your command, go on, shoot! And when it did, it found that it had hurt itself more than us. After that, capital, which is compelled to reckon with real political and economic life, says, "We must trade." ... Up to now they have not talked like this; up to now they said, "We will shoot you down and get you for nothing." Now since they are unable to shoot us, they are prepared to trade.[157]

3. The Party must always expect outside groups to violate agreements.

In 1920, Lenin said about the policy of granting economic "concessions" to foreign entrepreneurs:

Of course, the capitalists will not fulfil the agreements, say the comrades who fear concessions. That is a matter of course, one must absolutely not hope that the capitalists will fulfil the agreements.[158]

*   *   *

These attitudes imply that a "settlement" with the Western Powers—that is, an agreement sharply reducing the threat of mutual annihilation—is inconceivable to the Politburo, although arrangements with them, codifying the momentary relationship of forces, are always considered.

Footnotes

1. "X," "The Sources of Soviet Conduct," *Foreign Affairs*, July, 1947; Historicus, "Stalin on Revolution," *Foreign Affairs*, January, 1949.
2. *The Soviet-Yugoslav Dispute.*
3. V. I. Lenin, *Selected Works*, Vol. 8, p. 274.
4. *Ibid.*, Vol. 9, p. 335.
5. *History of the Communist Party of the Soviet Union (Bolsheviks). Short Course*, p. 334.
6. Lenin, *op. cit.*, Vol. 6, p. 512.
7. V. I. Lenin, *Sochineniya*, 3d ed., Vol. 30, p. 299.
8. V. I. Lenin, *Collected Works*, Vol. 23, p. 120.
9. *The Soviet-Yugoslav Dispute*, p. 45.
10. V. I. Lenin, *Selected Works*, Vol. 9, pp. 475–479.
11. Joseph Stalin, *Leninism*, Vol. 1, p. 416.
12. Joseph Stalin, *Leninism: Selected Writings*, p. 279.
13. *The Soviet-Yugoslav Dispute*, p. 31.
14. V. I. Lenin, *Selected Works*, Vol. 9, p. 355.
15. *Ibid.*, pp. 28–29.
16. *Ibid.*, Vol. 10, p. 71.
17. Joseph Stalin, *Sochineniya*, 4th ed., Vol. 8, p. 279.
18. Joseph Stalin, *Leninism*, Vol. 1, p. 379.
19. *History of the Communist Party of the Soviet Union (Bolsheviks). Short Course*, p. 411.
20. V. I. Lenin, *Collected Works*, Vol. 4, Book I, pp. 115–116.
21. Joseph Stalin, *Sochineniya*, Vol. 7, p. 68.
22. Joseph Stalin, *Leninism*, Vol. 1, pp. 217–255.
23. V. I. Lenin, *Selected Works*, Vol. 10, p. 48.
24. V. I. Lenin, *Sochineniya*, 4th ed., Vol. 13, p. 12.
25. *Ibid.*, Vol. 27, p. 146.
26. V. I. Lenin, *Selected Works*, Vol. 10, p. 104.
27. V. I. Lenin, *Collected Works*, Vol. 23, p. 196.
28. V. I. Lenin, *Selected Works*, Vol. 8, p. 290.
29. Joseph Stalin, *Leninism: Selected Writings*, pp. 295–296.
30. Joseph Stalin, *Leninism*, Vol. 2, p. 39.
31. *Ibid.*, p. 353.

32. Joseph Stalin, *Leninism: Selected Writings*, p. 205.
33. *Ibid.*, p. 225.
34. V. I. Lenin, *Sochineniya*, 4th ed., Vol. 13, p. 85.
35. W. P. and Z. K. Coates (comp.), *The Moscow Trial and Two Speeches by J. Stalin*, p. 261.
36. V. I. Lenin, *Selected Works*, Vol. 7, p. 300.
37. Joseph Stalin, *Leninism: Selected Writings*, pp. 354–355.
38. Joseph Stalin, *Sochineniya*, Vol. 8, p. 190.
39. V. I. Lenin, *Selected Works*, Vol. 10, pp. 103–105.
40. Joseph Stalin, *Leninism: Selected Writings*, p. 211.
41. V. I. Lenin, *Sochineniya*, 3d ed., Vol. 29, p. 247.
42. V. I. Lenin, *Selected Works*, Vol. 9, p. 198.
43. Joseph Stalin, *Sochineniya*, Vol. 10, p. 157.
44. V. I. Lenin, *Sochineniya*, 4th ed., Vol. 8, p. 206.
45. Joseph Stalin, *Leninism*, Vol. 1, p. 250.
46. V. I. Lenin, *Sochineniya*, 4th ed., Vol. 27, pp. 96–97.
47. Joseph Stalin, *Leninism*, Vol. 2, pp. 385–386.
48. V. I. Lenin, *Collected Works*, Vol. 4, Book II, pp. 244–245, 245n.
49. V. I. Lenin, *Selected Works*, Vol. 8, p. 31.
50. Joseph Stalin, *Sochineniya*, Vol. 5, pp. 220–221.
51. V. I. Lenin, *Collected Works*, Vol. 4, Book II, p. 201.
52. Joseph Stalin, *Leninism: Selected Writings*, p. 352.
53. Joseph Stalin, *Sochineniya*, Vol. 6, pp. 230–231.
54. V. I. Lenin, *Sochineniya*, 3d ed., Vol. 26, p. 200.
55. Joseph Stalin, *The Soviet Union and World Peace*, p. 9.
56. V. I. Lenin, *Selected Works*, Vol. 8, p. 39.
57. Joseph Stalin, *Marxism vs. Liberalism: An Interview [between] Joseph Stalin [and] H. G. Wells*, p. 3
58. Joseph Stalin, *Leninism*, Vol. 2, pp. 49–50.
59. *Ibid.*, Vol. 1, pp. 408–409.
60. Joseph Stalin, *Leninism: Selected Writings*, p. 444.
61. Joseph Stalin, *Sochineniya*, Vol. 9, p. 325.
62. Joseph Stalin, *Leninism: Selected Writings*, p. 279.
63. *Ibid.*, p. 76.
64. Joseph Stalin, *The October Revolution*, p. 154.
65. V. I. Lenin, *Sochineniya*, 4th ed., Vol. 6, p. 59.
66. Joseph Stalin, *Sochineniya*, Vol. 8, p. 361.
67. *Ibid.*, p. 341.
68. *History of the Communist Party of the Soviet Union (Bolsheviks). Short Course*, pp. 102–103.

69. V. I. Lenin, *Selected Works*, Vol. 9, p. 28.
70. V. I. Lenin, *Sochineniya*, 3d ed., Vol. 26, p. 180.
71. Joseph Stalin, *Leninism: Selected Writings*, p. 163.
72. V. I. Lenin, *Sochineniya*, 3d ed., Vol. 24, p. 291.
73. V. I. Lenin, *Selected Works*, Vol. 9, p. 242.
74. V. I. Lenin, *Sochineniya*, 4th ed., Vol. 27, p. 140.
75. V. I. Lenin, *Collected Works*, Vol. 23, pp. 122–123.
76. Joseph Stalin, *Marxism vs. Liberalism: An Interview [between]*
    Joseph Stalin [and] H. G. Wells, pp. 13–14.
77. V. I. Lenin, *Selected Works*, Vol. 9, p. 192.
78. Joseph Stalin, *Sochineniya*, Vol. 10, p. 46.
79. V. I. Lenin, *Sochineniya*, 4th ed., Vol. 26, p. 362.
80. Joseph Stalin, *Leninism*, Vol. 2, pp. 98–99.
81. *Ibid.*, Vol. 1, p. 223.
82. *Ibid.*, Vol. 2, p. 71.
83. V. I. Lenin, *Sochineniya*, 3d ed., Vol. 22, p. 259.
84. V. I. Lenin, *Collected Works*, Vol. 23, p. 230.
85. Joseph Stalin, *Leninism*, Vol. 1, p. 370.
86. V. I. Lenin, *Collected Works*, Vol. 23, p. 255.
87. V. I. Lenin, *Selected Works*, Vol. 8, pp. 279–280.
88. Joseph Stalin, *Marxism and the National Question*, pp. 104–105.
89. V. I. Lenin, *Selected Works*, Vol. 8, p. 284.
90. V. I. Lenin, *Sochineniya*, 3d ed., Vol. 26, p. 11.
91. Joseph Stalin, *Sochineniya*, Vol. 7, p. 14.
92. Joseph Stalin, *Leninism: Selected Writings*, p. 440.
93. V. I. Lenin, *Sochineniya*, 3d ed., Vol. 28, p. 143.
94. Joseph Stalin, *Leninism: Selected Writings*, p. 281.
95. V. I. Lenin, *Collected Works*, Vol. 23, pp. 336–337.
96. V. I. Lenin, *Selected Works*, Vol. 10, p. 233.
97. V. I. Lenin, *Sochineniya*, 3d ed., Vol. 26, p. 428.
98. Joseph Stalin, *Leninism*, Vol. 1, p. 280.
99. Joseph Stalin, *Leninism: Selected Writings*, p. 249.
100. V. I. Lenin, *Selected Works*, Vol. 8, p. 261.
101. Joseph Stalin, *Leninism: Selected Writings*, p. 268.
102. V. I. Lenin, *Selected Works*, Vol. 8, p. 264.
103. *Ibid.*, Vol. 10, p. 144.
104. *Ibid.*, Vol. 8, p. 321.
105. Joseph Stalin, *Leninism*, Vol. 1, pp. 220–222.
106. Joseph Stalin, *Sochineniya*, Vol. 10, p. 283.
107. V. I. Lenin, *Selected Works*, Vol. 8, pp. 275–276.
108. Joseph Stalin, *Sochineniya*, Vol. 6, p. 57.

109. *Ibid.*, Vol. 5, p. 167.
110. V. I. Lenin, *Sochineniya*, 3d ed., Vol. 30, p. 287.
111. V. I. Lenin, *Letters of Lenin*, p. 464.
112. Joseph Stalin, *Leninism: Selected Writings*, p. 184.
113. Joseph Stalin, *Sochineniya*, Vol. 9, pp. 325–328.
114. V. I. Lenin, *Sochineniya*, 4th ed., Vol. 26, p. 407.
115. *Ibid.*, 3d ed., Vol. 22, p. 201.
116. V. I. Lenin, *Selected Works*, Vol. 9, pp. 277–279.
117. *Ibid.*, pp. 284–285.
118. *Ibid.*, p. 313.
119. Joseph Stalin, *Foundations of Leninism*, pp. 102–103.
120. V. I. Lenin, *Sochineniya*, 3d ed., Vol. 28, p. 179.
121. *Ibid.*, p. 180.
122. Joseph Stalin, *Leninism: Selected Writings*, p. 70.
123. V. I. Lenin, *Sochineniya*, 4th ed., Vol. 7, p. 465.
124. *Ibid.*, Vol. 15, p. 42.
125. *Ibid.*, Vol. 8, pp. 50–51
126. *Ibid.*, Vol. 13, p. 100.
127. *Ibid.*, Vol. 6, p. 232.
128. *Ibid.*, Vol. 8, pp. 147–148.
129. Joseph Stalin, *Leninism*, Vol. 2, p. 98.
130. Joseph Stalin, *Leninism: Selected Writings*, p. 197.
131. *Ibid.*, p. 442.
132. *Ibid.*, pp. 129–130.
133. V. I. Lenin, *Letters of Lenin*, p. 202.
134. *History of the Communist Party of the Soviet Union (Bolsheviks). Short Course*, p. 196.
135. Joseph Stalin, *Leninism: Selected Writings*, p. 200.
136. *Ibid.*
137. V. I. Lenin, *Sochineniya*, 3d ed., Vol. 24, p. 291.
138. *Ibid.*, 2d ed., Vol. 25, pp. 298–299.
139. *Ibid.*, 3d ed., Vol. 27, p. 271.
140. *Ibid.*, 4th ed., Vol. 27, p. 134.
141. *Ibid.*, 3d ed., Vol. 27, p. 126.
142. V. I. Lenin, *Selected Works*, Vol. 9, p. 341.
143. V. I. Lenin, *Sochineniya*, 3d ed., Vol. 27, p. 78.
144. V. I. Lenin, *Selected Works*, Vol. 7, p. 297.
145. V. I. Lenin, *Sochineniya*, 4th ed., Vol. 27, p. 159.
146. Joseph Stalin, *Sochineniya*, Vol. 5, pp. 167–168.
147. V. I. Lenin, *Selected Works*, Vol. 7, p. 307.
148. V. I. Lenin, *Sochineniya*, 4th ed., Vol. 27, p. 52.

149. V. I. Lenin, *Selected Works*, Vol. 7, p. 294.
150. V. I. Lenin, *Sochineniya*, 4th ed., Vol. 27, p. 150.
151. V. I. Lenin, *Selected Works*, Vol. 9, p. 242.
152. V. I. Lenin, *Sochineniya*, 4th ed., Vol. 27, p. 135.
153. *Ibid.*, pp. 4–5.
154. V. I. Lenin, *Selected Works*, Vol. 9, pp. 291–293.
155. V. I. Lenin, *Sochineniya*, 3d ed., Vol. 26, p. 6.
156. V. I. Lenin, *Selected Works*, Vol. 8, p. 250.
157. *Ibid.*, Vol. 9, pp. 115–116.
158. V. I. Lenin, *Sochineniya*, 3d ed., Vol. 26, p. 22.

Bibliography

Bibliography

COATES, W. P., and Z. K. COATES (comp.), *The Moscow Trial and Two Speeches by J. Stalin*, Anglo-Russian Parliamentary Committee, London, 1937.

HISTORICUS, "Stalin on Revolution," *Foreign Affairs*, January, 1949.

History of the Communist Party of the Soviet Union (Bolsheviks). Short Course, edited by a Commission of the Central Committee of the CPSU(B), International Publishers, New York, 1939.

LENIN, V. I., *Collected Works*, International Publishers, New York.

———, *Letters of Lenin*, trans. and ed. by Elizabeth Hill and Doris Mudie, Harcourt, Brace and Company, Inc., New York, 1937.

———, *Selected Works*, International Publishers, New York.

———, *Sochineniya*, 2d ed., Institut Marksa-Engelsa-Lenina pri TsK VKP(b), Gosudarstvennoe Izdatelstvo Politicheskoi Literaturi, Moscow, 1926–32.

———, *Sochineniya*, 3d ed., Institut Marksa-Engelsa-Lenina pri TsK VKP(b), Gosudarstvennoe Izdatelstvo Politicheskoi Literaturi, Moscow, 1928–37.

———, *Sochineniya*, 4th ed., Institut Marksa-Engelsa-Lenina pri TsK VKP(b), Gosudarstvennoe Izdatelstvo Politicheskoi Literaturi, Moscow, 1941———.

The Soviet-Yugoslav Dispute, Royal Institute of International Affairs, London, 1948.

STALIN, JOSEPH, *Foundations of Leninism*, International Publishers, New York, 1932.

———, *Leninism*, Vols. 1 and 2, Modern Books, Ltd., London, 1932–33.

———, *Leninism: Selected Writings*, International Publishers, New York, 1942.

———, *Marxism and the National Question*, International Publishers, New York, 1942.

————, *Marxism vs. Liberalism, An Interview [between] Joseph Stalin [and] H. G. Wells*, New Century Publishers, New York, 1947.

————, *The October Revolution*, International Publishers, New York, 1934.

————, *The Soviet Union and World Peace*, New Century Publishers, New York, 1946.

————, *Sochineniya*, Institut Marksa-Engelsa-Lenina pri TsK VKP(b), Gosudarstvennoe Izdatelstvo Politicheskoi Literaturi, Moscow, 1948.

"X," "The Sources of Soviet Conduct," *Foreign Affairs*, July, 1947.

Index